D0007128

A gift for

_____

from

_____

THE TRAVELER'S GIFT
JOURNAL

Making the 7 Decisions for Personal Success
Your Story

BASED ON THE *NEW YORK TIMES*
BESTSELLING BOOK

by

ANDY ANDREWS

THOMAS NELSON
Since 1798

NASHVILLE   DALLAS   MEXICO CITY   RIO DE JANEIRO

Dedicated to Foncie and Joe Bullard whose determination to make a difference in the lives of others has been an inspiration to me.

© 2004 by Andy Andrews

All rights reserved. No portion of this book may be reproduced, stored in a retrieval system, or transmitted in any form or by any means—electronic, mechanical, photocopy, recording, scanning, or other—except for brief quotations in critical reviews or articles, without the prior written permission of the publisher.

Published in Nashville, Tennessee, by Thomas Nelson. Thomas Nelson is a registered trademark of Thomas Nelson, Inc.

Thomas Nelson, Inc., titles may be purchased in bulk for educational, business, fund-raising, or sales promotional use. For information, please e-mail SpecialMarkets@ThomasNelson.com.

Scripture quotations are taken from the HOLY BIBLE: NEW INTERNATIONAL VERSION®. © 1973, 1978, 1984 by International Bible Society. Used by permission of Zondervan Publishing House. All rights reserved.

ISBN 978.1-4041-7499-3 (revised)

Printed in the United States of America

10 11 12 13 14 RRD 5 4 3 2 1

Table of Contents

In great deed, something abides.
On great fields, something stays. Forms change
and pass, bodies disappear but spirits linger to
consecrate ground for the vision place of the
soul. And reverent men and women from afar
and generations that know us not and that we
know not of, shall come here to ponder and to
dream and the power of the vision shall pass
into their souls.

JOSHUA LAWRENCE CHAMBERLAIN, 1828–1914

Introduction for

THE TRAVELER'S GIFT JOURNAL

The Traveler's Gift had its beginnings more than twenty years ago when my parents died. My mother succumbed to a long battle with cancer; my father was killed in an automobile accident shortly thereafter. I was nineteen.

Like David Ponder, the protagonist of "The Traveler's Gift", I was plunged into the worst time in my very young life...and I did not respond well. Suffice it to say, I made a series of bad decisions, and through the course of the next several years managed to make an already bad situation even worse. For a period of time, I found myself quite literally homeless—and this was before "homeless" was even a word!

I was without a job, a car, or benefactor and frankly, it never occurred to me to apply for welfare or food stamps. I slept occasionally under a pier on the beach or sometimes in someone's garage. And I felt alone . . . quietly terrified . . . certain that God had conspired against me.

My question at the time was this: Is life just a lottery ticket? I wondered constantly whether happiness and success were the birthright of some and denied to others. Incidentally, I must admit, the thought crossed my mind that if I *did* determine that life *was* a lottery ticket—and if this was the ticket I held—I just might quit this miserable game altogether.

So I began to read. I eventually read more than two hundred biographies of happy, influential, contented, financially secure—personally successful—people. Why were they so different from me, I wondered? Were they born this way? Or were there choices made along the way that determined the direction and outcome of their lives?

In time, a pattern began to emerge. I identified seven things . . . seven common denominators in the lives of all these great people. There were quite obviously seven distinct characteristics that had been employed to create what the world now saw as enormously successful people. What would happen, I asked myself, if I put these seven principles to work in my own life? What would happen if I embraced these principles as seven distinct *decisions* to be studied, understood, and never to be reneged upon?

The answers to those questions began to weave the very fabric of my life. The journal you now hold in your hands was constructed in much the same way I made the seven decisions my own so many years ago. For twenty-one days, I pondered (and yes, that is how David got his name) each decision before moving on to the next. I graded myself every day on how well—or how poorly—I felt I had done. The Traveler's Gift Journal also includes daily questions to spark your imagination, some of which I asked myself during my own journey.

In closing, allow me to make one final, bold assertation: These Seven Decisions work every time! That's right, every single time. Why? Because they are principles. A decision is only a principle that you make your own. These are not seven theories or seven ideas. They are not even mine! Remember, I only identified them.

Principles always work. Even if one is unaware of a principle or ignores it—the principle continues to work. For example, the principle of gravity was working long before the apple ever fell on Newton's head. When it did, however, and he understood it, then we as a society were free to harness that principle to create, among other things, airline flight. The principles of personal success are exactly the same. They are within our grasp. Therefore, why shouldn't we learn these principles, harness them, and use them to create the future of our choosing!

Read each decision for twenty-one days—once upon awakening each morning and once before sleeping at night. Use these pages to keep your thoughts and vision firmly on the life you want to live. Grade yourself each day and honestly answer the questions posed about your attitude, actions, and beliefs.

I am excited about the journey you are about to begin. While others may suspect or hope that a person can travel from "nothing" to great personal success, I know it to be possible beyond the shadow of a doubt . . . because I have seen it done countless times. The life you choose will be one of joy, fulfillment, laughter, influence, and love. By taking these seven principles and making them decisions of your own . . . the future of your dreams is within your grasp!

ANDY ANDREWS
ORANGE BEACH, ALABAMA

The Seven Decisions for Personal Success

The Buck Stops Here

I ACCEPT RESPONSIBILITY FOR MY PAST. I CONTROL MY THOUGHTS.
I CONTROL MY EMOTIONS. I AM RESPONSIBLE FOR MY SUCCESS.
THE BUCK STOPS HERE.

I Will Seek Wisdom

I WILL BE A SERVANT TO OTHERS. I WILL LISTEN TO THE COUNSEL OF WISE MEN.
I WILL CHOOSE MY FRIENDS WITH CARE.
I WILL SEEK WISDOM.

I Am a Person of Action

I AM COURAGEOUS. I AM A LEADER. I SEIZE THIS MOMENT. I CHOOSE NOW.
I AM A PERSON OF ACTION.

I Have a Decided Heart

I WILL NOT WAIT. I AM PASSIONATE ABOUT MY VISION FOR THE FUTURE.
MY COURSE HAS BEEN CHARTED. MY DESTINY IS ASSURED.
I HAVE A DECIDED HEART.

Today I Will Choose to be Happy

I WILL GREET EACH DAY WITH LAUGHTER. I WILL SMILE AT EVERY PERSON I
MEET. I AM THE POSSESSOR OF A GRATEFUL SPIRIT.
TODAY I WILL CHOOSE TO BE HAPPY.

I Will Greet This Day With a Forgiving Spirit

I WILL FORGIVE EVEN THOSE WHO DO NOT ASK FOR FORGIVENESS. I WILL
FORGIVE THOSE WHO CRITICIZE ME UNJUSTLY. I WILL FORGIVE MYSELF.
I WILL GREET THIS DAY WITH A FORGIVING SPIRIT.

I Will Persist Without Exception

I WILL CONTINUE DESPITE EXHAUSTION. I FOCUS ON RESULTS.
I AM A PERSON OF GREAT FAITH.
I WILL PERSIST WITHOUT EXCEPTION.

The Responsible Decision for Success
THE BUCK STOPS HERE.

From this moment forward, I will accept responsibility for my past. I understand that the beginning of wisdom is to accept the responsibility for my own problems and that by accepting responsibility for my past, I free myself to move into a bigger, brighter future of my own choosing.

Never again will I blame my parents, my spouse, my boss, or other employees for my present situation. Neither my education nor lack of one, my genetics, or the circumstantial ebb and flow of everyday life will affect my future in a negative way. If I allow myself to blame these uncontrollable forces for my lack of success, I will be forever caught in a web of the past. I will look forward. I will not let my history control my destiny.

The buck stops here. I accept responsibility for my past. I am responsible for my success. I am where I am today—mentally, physically, spiritually, emotionally, and financially—because of decisions I have made. My decisions have always been governed by my thinking. Therefore, I am where I am today—mentally, physically, spiritually, emotionally, and financially—because of how I think. Today I will begin the process of changing where I am—mentally, physically, spiritually, emotionally, and financially—by changing the way I think.

My thoughts will be constructive, never destructive. My mind will live in the solutions of the future. It will not dwell in the problems of the past. I will seek the association of those who are working and striving to

1

bring about positive changes in the world. I will never seek comfort by associating with those who have decided to be comfortable.

When faced with the opportunity to make a decision, I will make one. I understand that God did not put in me the ability to always make right decisions. He did, however, put in me the ability to *make* a decision and then *make it right*. The rise and fall of my emotional tide will not deter me from my course. When I make a decision, I will stand behind it. My energy will go into making the decision. I will waste none on second thoughts. My life will not be an apology. It will be a statement.

The buck stops here. I control my thoughts. I control my emotions.

In the future when I am tempted to ask the question "Why me?" I will immediately counter with the answer: "Why *not* me?" Challenges are gifts, opportunities to learn. Problems are the common thread running through the lives of great men and women. In times of adversity, I will not have a problem to deal with; I will have a choice to make. My thoughts will be clear. I will make the right choice. Adversity is preparation for greatness. I will accept this preparation. Why me? Why *not* me? I will be prepared for something great!

I accept responsibility for my past.

I control my thoughts. I control my emotions.

I am responsible for my success.

The buck stops here.

I ACCEPT RESPONSIBILITY FOR MY PAST. I CONTROL MY THOUGHTS. I CONTROL MY
EMOTIONS. I AM RESPONSIBLE FOR MY SUCCESS. THE BUCK STOPS HERE.

How are you like David? What serpents are squeezing you?

From *The Traveler's Gift . . .*

D aniel felt panic enter
his very soul. Like a
serpent easing up his spine
and wrapping itself around
his throat, it wasn't a
quick, devastating attack,
but a slow, gripping realization that life, as he
knew it, was over. He was
forty-six years old. he had
no job. He had no money.
He had no purpose.

I have read the first decision for success today.   ☐ A.M.   ☐ P.M.

In applying this decision, today I would give myself a grade of: **A B C D**

I ACCEPT RESPONSIBILITY FOR MY PAST. I CONTROL MY THOUGHTS. I CONTROL MY
EMOTIONS. I AM RESPONSIBLE FOR MY SUCCESS. THE BUCK STOPS HERE.

What brings panic to your soul?
How do you work through such realizations?

_____

_____

_____

_____

_____

_____

_____

_____

_____

_____

_____

_____

_____

_____

_____

_____

_____

_____

_____

_____

_____

I have read the first decision for success today.   ☐ A.M.   ☐ P.M.

In applying this decision, today I would give myself a grade of: **A B C D**

I ACCEPT RESPONSIBILITY FOR MY PAST. I CONTROL MY THOUGHTS. I CONTROL MY EMOTIONS. I AM RESPONSIBLE FOR MY SUCCESS. THE BUCK STOPS HERE.

What have you promised to the people who love you?

From *The Traveler's Gift* . . .

A t one point, David remembered, he had taken Ellen's face in his hands and said, "I promise you everything," and she had not laughed. He had been serious, and she knew it.

I have read the first decision for success today.   ☐ A.M.   ☐ P.M.

In applying this decision, today I would give myself a grade of: **A B C D**

I ACCEPT RESPONSIBILITY FOR MY PAST. I CONTROL MY THOUGHTS. I CONTROL MY EMOTIONS. I AM RESPONSIBLE FOR MY SUCCESS. THE BUCK STOPS HERE.

How well are you keeping those promises made to the people you love?

_____

_____

_____

_____

_____

_____

_____

_____

_____

_____

_____

_____

_____

_____

_____

_____

_____

_____

_____

_____

I have read the first decision for success today.   ☐ A.M.   ☐ P.M.

In applying this decision, today I would give myself a grade of: **A B C D**

I ACCEPT RESPONSIBILITY FOR MY PAST. I CONTROL MY THOUGHTS. I CONTROL MY EMOTIONS. I AM RESPONSIBLE FOR MY SUCCESS. THE BUCK STOPS HERE.

Think about what David said. Are you working so hard to live up to a certain standard to the detriment of what is really important in life?

From *The Traveler's Gift* . . .

David told a friend one day, "I'm working so hard to live where we want to live that I don't actually get to live there."

I have read the first decision for success today.   ☐ A.M.   ☐ P.M.

In applying this decision, today I would give myself a grade of: **A B C D**

I ACCEPT RESPONSIBILITY FOR MY PAST. I CONTROL MY THOUGHTS. I CONTROL MY EMOTIONS. I AM RESPONSIBLE FOR MY SUCCESS. THE BUCK STOPS HERE.

How is the pressure to keep up taking its toll on you?
C'mon, be honest. What are you missing?

_____

_____

_____

_____

_____

_____

_____

_____

_____

_____

_____

_____

_____

_____

_____

_____

_____

_____

_____

_____

_____

I have read the first decision for success today.   ☐ A.M.   ☐ P.M.

In applying this decision, today I would give myself a grade of: **A B C D**

Truth be known, God is interested in what you never dare to say. Sure, God knows what you keep to yourself, but he'd really like to hear you say it. Just once. Go ahead. Show him your hand, and speak your peace.

From *The Traveler's Gift* . . .

David pulled onto the shoulder. Bowing his head, he clasped his hands together. "Oh, God," he said aloud. "Oh, God . . ." He stopped and was silent for almost a minute. "Oh, God . . . ," he began again. After another minute, he put the Colt into gear and moved back onto the highway. I can't even pray, he thought.

I have read the first decision for success today.   ☐ A.M.   ☐ P.M.

In applying this decision, today I would give myself a grade of: **A B C D**

I ACCEPT RESPONSIBILITY FOR MY PAST. I CONTROL MY THOUGHTS. I CONTROL MY EMOTIONS. I AM RESPONSIBLE FOR MY SUCCESS. THE BUCK STOPS HERE.

Have you ever wished you were someone, anyone else but you?
What made you feel that way?

From *The Traveler's Gift* . . .

Y ou're Harry Truman," David said in a shocked tone.

"Yes," the man said, "I am. Though at the moment I would give anything to be almost anyone else."

Swallowing audibly, David said, "They call you 'Give 'Em Hell Harry.'"

Truman grimaced. "I never give anybody hell," he snorted. "I just tell the truth, and they think it's hell."

I have read the first decision for success today.   ☐ A.M.   ☐ P.M.

In applying this decision, today I would give myself a grade of: **A B C D**

I ACCEPT RESPONSIBILITY FOR MY PAST. I CONTROL MY THOUGHTS. I CONTROL MY EMOTIONS. I AM RESPONSIBLE FOR MY SUCCESS. THE BUCK STOPS HERE.

When you feel the lowest,
who can you count on to tell you the truth?

_____

_____

_____

_____

_____

_____

_____

_____

_____

_____

_____

_____

_____

_____

_____

_____

_____

_____

_____

I have read the first decision for success today. ☐ A.M. ☐ P.M.

In applying this decision, today I would give myself a grade of: **A B C D**

I ACCEPT RESPONSIBILITY FOR MY PAST. I CONTROL MY THOUGHTS. I CONTROL MY
EMOTIONS. I AM RESPONSIBLE FOR MY SUCCESS. THE BUCK STOPS HERE.

Instead of asking 'Why, me?' try asking,
'What is the value I'm supposed to take away from this
situation?' Now try answering that one.

From *The Traveler's Gift* . . .

W hy . . . not . . . you?"
Looking directly
into David's eyes, he
enunciated the words
carefully, separating them as
if he were speaking to a
child. "I believe that is the
answer to the last question
you asked before you
arrived. 'Why me?' is a
question great men and
women have been asking
themselves since time
began."

I have read the first decision for success today.   ☐ A.M.   ☐ P.M.

In applying this decision, today I would give myself a grade of: **A B C D**

I ACCEPT RESPONSIBILITY FOR MY PAST. I CONTROL MY THOUGHTS. I CONTROL MY
EMOTIONS. I AM RESPONSIBLE FOR MY SUCCESS. THE BUCK STOPS HERE.

*If God believes in you, and there is much evidence to support that
God does, then one can hardly argue that you are ordinary. After
all, there is nothing ordinary about anything in creation, most of
all you. As sure as you are you, in God's eyes (by his grace) you
are great. List three blessings or gifts God has bestowed on you.*

From *The Traveler's Gift* . . .

B ut I'm an ordinary
guy," David said. "I'm
nothing like any of the
people you've mentioned—
great, I mean—and I'm
certainly no apostle Paul.
I'm not even sure I believe
in God anymore."

Truman smiled as he put
a hand on David's shoulder.
"That's all right, son," he
said. "He believes in you."

I have read the first decision for success today.   ☐ A.M.   ☐ P.M.

In applying this decision, today I would give myself a grade of: **A B C D**

I ACCEPT RESPONSIBILITY FOR MY PAST. I CONTROL MY THOUGHTS. I CONTROL MY EMOTIONS. I AM RESPONSIBLE FOR MY SUCCESS. THE BUCK STOPS HERE.

When you hear the word 'choice,' what do you think of?

From *The Traveler's Gift* . . .

T he ultimate outcome of anyone's life is a matter of personal choice," Truman said.

"This is the essence of why you are here. It is one of the Decisions for Success."

_____

_____

_____

_____

_____

_____

_____

_____

_____

_____

_____

_____

_____

_____

_____

_____

_____

_____

_____

_____

_____

_____

I have read the first decision for success today.   ☐ A.M.   ☐ P.M.

In applying this decision, today I would give myself a grade of: **A B C D**

I ACCEPT RESPONSIBILITY FOR MY PAST. I CONTROL MY THOUGHTS. I CONTROL MY
EMOTIONS. I AM RESPONSIBLE FOR MY SUCCESS. THE BUCK STOPS HERE.

Historically, have you made wise choices?
Write down the wisest choice you ever made.

_____

_____

_____

_____

_____

_____

_____

_____

_____

_____

_____

_____

_____

_____

_____

_____

_____

_____

_____

_____

_____

I have read the first decision for success today.   ☐ A.M.   ☐ P.M.

In applying this decision, today I would give myself a grade of: **A B C D**

I ACCEPT RESPONSIBILITY FOR MY PAST. I CONTROL MY THOUGHTS. I CONTROL MY EMOTIONS. I AM RESPONSIBLE FOR MY SUCCESS. THE BUCK STOPS HERE.

Think about the biggest decision you have made to date. The absolute, no-going-back decision. Who or what influenced that decision?

From *The Traveler's Gift* . . .

Outside influences are not responsible for where you are mentally, physically, spiritually, emotionally, or financially. You have chosen the pathway to your present destination. The responsibility for your situation is yours.

_____
_____
_____
_____
_____
_____
_____
_____
_____
_____
_____
_____
_____
_____
_____
_____
_____
_____
_____
_____
_____
_____
_____

I have read the first decision for success today.   ☐ A.M.   ☐ P.M.

In applying this decision, today I would give myself a grade of: **A B C D**

I ACCEPT RESPONSIBILITY FOR MY PAST. I CONTROL MY THOUGHTS. I CONTROL MY EMOTIONS. I AM RESPONSIBLE FOR MY SUCCESS. THE BUCK STOPS HERE.

How has that one decision changed
the trajectory your life?

_____

_____

_____

_____

_____

_____

_____

_____

_____

_____

_____

_____

_____

_____

_____

_____

_____

_____

_____

_____

I have read the first decision for success today.   ☐ A.M.   ☐ P.M.

In applying this decision, today I would give myself a grade of: **A B C D**

I ACCEPT RESPONSIBILITY FOR MY PAST. I CONTROL MY THOUGHTS. I CONTROL MY
EMOTIONS. I AM RESPONSIBLE FOR MY SUCCESS. THE BUCK STOPS HERE.

When was the last time you used those famous words?

From *The Traveler's Gift* . . .

The words "It's not my fault! "have been symbolically written on the gravestones of unsuccessful people ever since Eve took her first bite of the apple. Until a person takes responsibility for where he is, there is no basis for moving on.

I have read the first decision for success today.   ☐ A.M.   ☐ P.M.

In applying this decision, today I would give myself a grade of: **A B C D**

I ACCEPT RESPONSIBILITY FOR MY PAST. I CONTROL MY THOUGHTS. I CONTROL MY EMOTIONS. I AM RESPONSIBLE FOR MY SUCCESS. THE BUCK STOPS HERE.

What was the poor choice behind those words?

_____

_____

_____

_____

_____

_____

_____

_____

_____

_____

_____

_____

_____

_____

_____

_____

_____

_____

_____

I have read the first decision for success today.   ☐ A.M.   ☐ P.M.

In applying this decision, today I would give myself a grade of: **A B C D**

I ACCEPT RESPONSIBILITY FOR MY PAST. I CONTROL MY THOUGHTS. I CONTROL MY EMOTIONS. I AM RESPONSIBLE FOR MY SUCCESS. THE BUCK STOPS HERE.

The downside of 'choice' is the possibility of making the wrong one. What destructive thoughts do you need to overcome concerning a bad choice?

From *The Traveler's Gift* . . .

A nd one more thing," Truman said. "Just because I use the expression 'good luck' doesn't mean that luck actually has anything to do with where you end up."

_____

_____

_____

_____

_____

_____

_____

_____

_____

_____

_____

_____

_____

_____

_____

_____

_____

_____

_____

_____

_____

I have read the first decision for success today.   ☐ A.M.   ☐ P.M.

In applying this decision, today I would give myself a grade of: **A B C D**

I ACCEPT RESPONSIBILITY FOR MY PAST. I CONTROL MY THOUGHTS. I CONTROL MY
EMOTIONS. I AM RESPONSIBLE FOR MY SUCCESS. THE BUCK STOPS HERE.

*The downside of luck is that if it exists at all, it runs out way
too fast. Who is the luckiest person you know?
Why is he or she 'lucky'? What choices might be
hiding behind that 'luck'?*

_____

_____

_____

_____

_____

_____

_____

_____

_____

_____

_____

_____

_____

_____

_____

_____

_____

_____

_____

I have read the first decision for success today.   ☐ A.M.   ☐ P.M.

In applying this decision, today I would give myself a grade of: **A B C D**

I ACCEPT RESPONSIBILITY FOR MY PAST. I CONTROL MY THOUGHTS. I CONTROL MY
EMOTIONS. I AM RESPONSIBLE FOR MY SUCCESS. THE BUCK STOPS HERE.

*"To know where you're going," someone wise once said, "you've
got to know where you've been." She didn't say ". . . and you'd
better stay there." What part of your past do you need to put
behind you for good, in order to take hold of the future?*

From *The Traveler's Gift* . . .

"The bad news," Truman
told David, "is that the
past was in your hands, but
the good news is that the
future, my friend, is also in
your hands."

_____

_____

_____

_____

_____

_____

_____

_____

_____

_____

_____

_____

_____

_____

_____

_____

_____

_____

_____

_____

I have read the first decision for success today.   ☐ A.M.   ☐ P.M.

In applying this decision, today I would give myself a grade of: **A B C D**

I ACCEPT RESPONSIBILITY FOR MY PAST. I CONTROL MY THOUGHTS. I CONTROL MY EMOTIONS. I AM RESPONSIBLE FOR MY SUCCESS. THE BUCK STOPS HERE.

Am I really seeking to work towards positive change? Am I seeking out those people who are also working towards positive change?

I have read the first decision for success today.   ☐ A.M.   ☐ P.M.

In applying this decision, today I would give myself a grade of: **A B C D**

I ACCEPT RESPONSIBILITY FOR MY PAST. I CONTROL MY THOUGHTS. I CONTROL MY EMOTIONS. I AM RESPONSIBLE FOR MY SUCCESS. THE BUCK STOPS HERE.

The Responsible Decision
"The Buck Stops Here"
Write this decision in your own words.

I have read the first decision for success today.   ☐ A.M.   ☐ P.M.

In applying this decision, today I would give myself a grade of: **A B C D**

I ACCEPT RESPONSIBILITY FOR MY PAST. I CONTROL MY THOUGHTS. I CONTROL MY EMOTIONS. I AM RESPONSIBLE FOR MY SUCCESS. THE BUCK STOPS HERE.

Now express how this decision will change your life.

_____

_____

_____

_____

_____

_____

_____

_____

_____

_____

_____

_____

_____

_____

_____

_____

_____

_____

_____

_____

_____

I have read the first decision for success today.   ☐ A.M.   ☐ P.M.

In applying this decision, today I would give myself a grade of: **A B C D**

The Guided Decision for Success

I WILL SEEK WISDOM.

Knowing that wisdom waits to be gathered, I will actively search her out. My past can never be changed, but I can change the future by changing my actions today. I *will* change my actions today! I will train my eyes and ears to read and listen to books and recordings that bring about positive changes in my personal relationships and a greater understanding of my fellowman. No longer will I bombard my mind with materials that feed my doubts and fears. I will read and listen only to what increases my belief in myself and my future.

I will seek wisdom. I will choose my friends with care. I am who my friends are. I speak their language, and I wear their clothes. I share their opinions and their habits. From this moment forward, I will choose to associate with people whose lives and lifestyles I admire. If I associate with chickens, I will learn to scratch at the ground and squabble over crumbs. If I associate with eagles, I will learn to soar to great heights. I am an eagle. It is my destiny to fly.

I will seek wisdom. I will listen to the counsel of wise men. The words of a wise man are like raindrops on dry ground. They are precious and can be quickly used for immediate results. Only the blade of grass that catches a raindrop will prosper and grow. The person who ignores wise counsel is like the blade of grass untouched by the rain—soon to wither and die. When I counsel with just myself, I can make decisions only according to what I already know. By counseling with a wise man, I add his knowledge and experience to my own and dramatically increase my success.

I will seek wisdom. I will be a servant to others. A wise man will cultivate a servant's spirit, for that particular attribute attracts people like no other. As I humbly serve others, their wisdom will be freely shared with me. Often, the person who develops a servant's spirit becomes wealthy beyond measure. Many times, a servant has the ear of the king, and a humble servant often becomes a king, for he is the popular choice of the people. He who serves the most grows the fastest.

I will become a humble servant. I will not look for someone to open my door—I will look to open the door for someone. I will not be distressed when no one is available to help me—I will be excited when I am available to help.

I will be a servant to others.

I will listen to the counsel of wise men.

I will choose my friends with care.

I will seek wisdom.

27

I WILL BE A SERVANT TO OTHERS. I WILL SEEK WISDOM.

To be successful in anything, you have to be prepared to move when the opportunity presents itself. Are you willing and prepared to move, to make changes in your life?

From *The Traveler's Gift* . . .

How am I supposed to pass this . . . this gift to anyone?" David asked [King Solomon], shaking his head.

"That is something you may not know for yet some time. Then again, the answer could be revealed to you tomorrow. Jehovah moves mountains to create the opportunity of His choosing. It is up to you to be ready to move yourself."

I have read the second decision for success today.   ☐ A.M.   ☐ P.M.

In applying this decision, today I would give myself a grade of: **A B C D**

I WILL BE A SERVANT TO OTHERS. I WILL SEEK WISDOM.

Are you willing and prepared
to make even the tough changes?

_____

_____

_____

_____

_____

_____

_____

_____

_____

_____

_____

_____

_____

_____

_____

_____

_____

_____

_____

_____

I have read the second decision for success today.   ☐ A.M.   ☐ P.M.

In applying this decision, today I would give myself a grade of: **A B C D**

I WILL BE A SERVANT TO OTHERS. I WILL SEEK WISDOM.

Did you ever take a pop quiz? You know, those impromptu tests gleeful teachers spring on students, just for their own amusement? Now imagine that right now you're sitting for a pop quiz about a subject you know absolutely nothing about? How would that make you feel?

From *The Traveler's Gift* . . .

"Then here's a question," David said, almost sarcastically. "How do I prepare for something when I don't know (a) what it is or (b) when it will happen?"

"How do I prepare for an uncertain future?"

"Seek wisdom," the king said simply.

_____

_____

_____

_____

_____

_____

_____

_____

_____

_____

_____

_____

_____

_____

_____

_____

_____

_____

_____

I have read the second decision for success today.   ☐ A.M.   ☐ P.M.

In applying this decision, today I would give myself a grade of: **A B C D**

On a scale of 1 to 10, (one being 'not at all' and ten being 'perfectly so') rate your own DQ—your Diligence Quotient. Give yourself high marks for ears that hear more than a mouth that speaks and for persistence.

From *The Traveler's Gift* . . .

S eek wisdom. Seek
wisdom. Wisdom waits
to be gathered. She cannot
be bartered or sold. She is a
gift for the diligent. And
only the diligent will find
her. . . .

I have read the second decision for success today. ☐ A.M. ☐ P.M.

In applying this decision, today I would give myself a grade of: **A B C D**

I WILL BE A SERVANT TO OTHERS. I WILL SEEK WISDOM.

Who do you listen to when seeking the counsel of wise men?
Anyone else needing to be added to that list?

_____

_____

_____

_____

_____

_____

_____

_____

_____

_____

_____

_____

_____

_____

_____

_____

_____

_____

_____

_____

I have read the second decision for success today.   ☐ A.M.   ☐ P.M.

In applying this decision, today I would give myself a grade of: **A B C D**

I WILL BE A SERVANT TO OTHERS. I WILL SEEK WISDOM.

Now, go back to that DQ score. Divide your score by 2 if you tend to stay in your own comfort zone. Add 3 points if you're a risk-taker. Now what is your DQ?

From *The Traveler's Gift* . . .

The lazy man—the stupid man—never even looks. Though wisdom is available to many, she is found by few. Find her, and you will find success and contentment.

I have read the second decision for success today.   ☐ A.M.   ☐ P.M.

In applying this decision, today I would give myself a grade of: **A B C D**

I WILL BE A SERVANT TO OTHERS. I WILL SEEK WISDOM.

Take a "Present to Past" inventory: list five things in your present life circumstances that you would like to see fade to the past as quickly as possible?

From *The Traveler's Gift* . . .

W ell," David said, "I certainly don't have success or contentment in my life right now."

"All a part of the past," Solomon noted. "Even the present is constantly becoming the past—now . . . and now . . . and now." He snapped his fingers as he talked.

I have read the second decision for success today. ☐ A.M. ☐ P.M.

In applying this decision, today I would give myself a grade of: **A B C D**

How do you feel about 'change'? Do you naturally embrace it? Do you fear or dread it?

From *The Traveler's Gift* . . .

The past will never change, but you can change the future by changing your actions today. It is really a very simple process. We, as humans, are always in a process of change. Therefore, we might as well guide the direction in which we change.

I have read the second decision for success today.   ☐ A.M.   ☐ P.M.

In applying this decision, today I would give myself a grade of: **A B C D**

I WILL BE A SERVANT TO OTHERS. I WILL SEEK WISDOM.

*What was the last big change in your life
and how did you approach or react to it?*

_____

_____

_____

_____

_____

_____

_____

_____

_____

_____

_____

_____

_____

_____

_____

_____

_____

_____

I have read the second decision for success today.   ☐ A.M.   ☐ P.M.

In applying this decision, today I would give myself a grade of: **A B C D**

I WILL BE A SERVANT TO OTHERS. I WILL SEEK WISDOM.

What kind of friends did you have in junior high,
high school or college? How did they influence you?
(Drag out the yearbook if you have to.)

From *The Traveler's Gift* . . .

H ow do I guide the
direction in which I
change?" David asked.
    "How do you guide the
direction in which your
daughter changes?"
Solomon asked.
    "By keeping tabs on who
her friends are," David said.
    "Exactly!" the king
said excitedly.

I have read the second decision for success today.   ☐ A.M.   ☐ P.M.

In applying this decision, today I would give myself a grade of: **A B C D**

I WILL BE A SERVANT TO OTHERS. I WILL SEEK WISDOM.

Who was the most influential person in your life when you were 10? What about 21? What about now? Their impact lives on long after they're gone.

From *The Traveler's Gift* . . .

A nd at what age are we no longer affected by those around us? Eighteen? Twenty-one? Thirty? The answer, of course, is that we are always and forever influenced by those with whom we associate.

_____
_____
_____
_____
_____
_____
_____

_____
_____
_____
_____
_____
_____
_____
_____
_____
_____
_____

I have read the second decision for success today.   ☐ A.M.   ☐ P.M.

In applying this decision, today I would give myself a grade of: **A B C D**

I WILL BE A SERVANT TO OTHERS. I WILL SEEK WISDOM.

"You make me want to be a better man," says the obsessive/compulsive, best-selling author to his would-be waitress girlfriend in the movie "As Good As It Gets." Have you ever felt that way about someone in your life, someone who made you feel like a better person just for knowing him or her?

From *The Traveler's Gift* . . .

I f a man keeps company with those who curse and complain—he will soon find curses and complaints flowing like a river from his own mouth. If he spends his days with the lazy—those seeking handouts—he will soon find his finances in disarray. Many of our sorrows can be traced to relationships with the wrong people.

I have read the second decision for success today. ☐ A.M. ☐ P.M.

In applying this decision, today I would give myself a grade of: **A B C D**

I WILL BE A SERVANT TO OTHERS. I WILL SEEK WISDOM.

Do you think anyone thinks of you that way? Has your influence in someone's life made them a better person?

_____

_____

_____

_____

_____

_____

_____

_____

_____

_____

_____

_____

_____

_____

_____

_____

_____

_____

_____

_____

_____

I have read the second decision for success today.   ☐ A.M.   ☐ P.M.

In applying this decision, today I would give myself a grade of: **A B C D**

I WILL BE A SERVANT TO OTHERS. I WILL SEEK WISDOM.

In what areas of your life has mediocrity become the norm? You know, those areas where 'just getting' by' is 'good enough.'

From *The Traveler's Gift* . . .

D avid got to his feet. Wiping his hands on his jeans, he said, "So this is an important step in seeking wisdom?"

"Possibly the most important step," Solomon responded. "Guard your associations carefully, David. Anytime you tolerate mediocrity in your choice of companions, you become more comfortable with mediocrity in your own life."

I have read the second decision for success today.   ☐ A.M.   ☐ P.M.

In applying this decision, today I would give myself a grade of: **A B C D**

I WILL BE A SERVANT TO OTHERS. I WILL SEEK WISDOM.

Are there people in your life that have helped feed that "getting by is good enough" attitude? How are you striving to guard your associations?

I have read the second decision for success today.   ☐ A.M.   ☐ P.M.

In applying this decision, today I would give myself a grade of: **A B C D**

I WILL BE A SERVANT TO OTHERS. I WILL SEEK WISDOM.

One way to get where you want to be, to achieve the goals you want to achieve, is to find someone who's already there. Who is that person in your life?

From *The Traveler's Gift* . . .

You are the wisest man in the world," David said, "and obviously the richest. Yet you said you keep counsel with those other men. Why?"

Solomon smiled patiently. "Only a fool refuses the counsel of wise men. There is safety in counsel. Sensible instruction is a life-giving fountain that will help you escape all manner of deadly traps. Find a wise man, a person who has accomplished what you wish for in your own life, and listen closely to his words."

I have read the second decision for success today.   □ A.M.   □ P.M.

In applying this decision, today I would give myself a grade of: **A B C D**

I WILL BE A SERVANT TO OTHERS. I WILL SEEK WISDOM.

Are there ways to tap into that source,
to learn from that person?

_____

_____

_____

_____

_____

_____

_____

_____

_____

_____

_____

_____

_____

_____

_____

_____

_____

_____

_____

_____

I have read the second decision for success today.   ☐ A.M.   ☐ P.M.

In applying this decision, today I would give myself a grade of: **A B C D**

I WILL BE A SERVANT TO OTHERS. I WILL SEEK WISDOM.

Henry V, one of England's most revered kings, was loved not only for his military successes and diplomacy, but also for his consideration and service toward his subjects. Because he led with the spirit of a servant, they followed him against overwhelming odds. Write down one thing you can do today to show someone how much you value him or her. Then prove your wisdom by doing it.

From *The Traveler's Gift* . . .

When a king begins to act like a king, it is not long before someone else is king! Serving is a way we can place value on one another. A wise man is a server.

_____

I have read the second decision for success today.   ☐ A.M.   ☐ P.M.

In applying this decision, today I would give myself a grade of: **A B C D**

I WILL BE A SERVANT TO OTHERS. I WILL SEEK WISDOM.

What can you gain by being a servant to others?

_____

_____

_____

_____

_____

_____

_____

_____

_____

_____

_____

_____

_____

_____

_____

_____

_____

_____

_____

_____

_____

I have read the second decision for success today.   ☐ A.M.   ☐ P.M.

In applying this decision, today I would give myself a grade of: **A B C D**

Most new mothers agree that once they hold that squirmy, crying bundle of baby in their arms, the horrific pain of childbirth becomes a distant memory. Think about that when the up-hill climb has knocked you off your feet for the 18th time. Think about what that bright, brilliant future has in store for you. Can you get back up now? Can you try?

From *The Traveler's Gift* . . .

I can do nothing to alleviate your struggles and would not if I were able," Solomon said to David Ponder. "It is never the duty of a leader to struggle for someone else; a leader must encourage others to struggle and assure them that the struggles are worthwhile. Do battle with the challenges of your present, and you will unlock the prizes of your future."

I have read the second decision for success today.   ☐ A.M.   ☐ P.M.

In applying this decision, today I would give myself a grade of: **A B C D**

I WILL BE A SERVANT TO OTHERS. I WILL SEEK WISDOM.

What gave you the desire to get back up and soar like the eagle?
Do you realize your destiny is to fly?

I have read the second decision for success today.　☐ A.M.　☐ P.M.

In applying this decision, today I would give myself a grade of: **A B C D**

I WILL BE A SERVANT TO OTHERS. I WILL SEEK WISDOM.

The Guided Decision
"I Will Seek Wisdom"
Write this decision in your own words.

_____

_____

_____

_____

_____

_____

_____

_____

_____

_____

_____

_____

_____

_____

_____

_____

_____

_____

_____

I have read the second decision for success today.   ☐ A.M.   ☐ P.M.

In applying this decision, today I would give myself a grade of: **A B C D**

I WILL BE A SERVANT TO OTHERS. I WILL SEEK WISDOM.

Now express how this decision will change your life.

_____

_____

_____

_____

_____

_____

_____

_____

_____

_____

_____

_____

_____

_____

_____

_____

_____

_____

_____

_____

I have read the second decision for success today.   ☐ A.M.   ☐ P.M.

In applying this decision, today I would give myself a grade of: **A B C D**

The Active Decision for Success

I AM A PERSON OF ACTION.

Beginning today, I will create a new future by creating a new me. No longer will I dwell in a pit of despair, moaning over squandered time and lost opportunity. I can do nothing about the past. My future is immediate. I will grasp it in both hands and carry it with running feet. When I am faced with the choice of doing nothing or doing something, I will always choose to act! I seize this moment. I choose now.

I am a person of action. I am energetic. I move quickly. Knowing that laziness is a sin, I will create a habit of lively behavior. I will walk with a spring in my step and a smile on my face. The lifeblood rushing through my veins is urging me upward and forward into activity and accomplishment. Wealth and prosperity hide from the sluggard, but rich rewards come to the person who moves quickly.

I am a person of action. I inspire others with my activity. I am a leader. Leading is doing. To lead, I must move forward. Many people move out of the way for a person on the run; others are caught up in his wake. My activity will create a wave of success for the people who follow. My activity will be consistent. This will instill confidence in my leadership. As a leader, I have the ability to encourage and inspire others to greatness. It is true: an army of sheep led by a lion would defeat an army of lions led by a sheep.

I am a person of action. I can make a decision. I can make it now. A person who moves neither left nor right is destined for mediocrity.

When faced with a decision, many people say they are waiting for God. But I understand, in most cases, God is waiting for me! He has given me a healthy mind to gather and sort information and the courage to come to a conclusion. I am not a quivering dog, indecisive and fearful. My constitution is strong and my pathway clear. Successful people make their decisions quickly and change their minds slowly. Failures make their decisions slowly and change their minds quickly. My decisions come quickly, and they lead to victory.

I am a person of action. I am daring. I am courageous. Fear no longer has a place in my life. For too long, fear has outweighed my desire to make things better for my family. Never again! I have exposed fear as a vapor, an impostor that never had any power over me in the first place! I do not fear opinion, gossip, or the idle chatter of monkeys, for all are the same to me. I do not fear failure, for in my life, failure is a myth. Failure exists only for the person who quits. I do not quit.

I am courageous.

I am a leader.

I seize this moment.

I choose now.

I am a person of action.

I SEIZE THIS MOMENT. I CHOOSE NOW. I AM A PERSON OF ACTION.

Sometimes doing the right thing is the hardest thing. Write about a time in your life when you made the difficult choice to do the honorable thing.

From *The Traveler's Gift* . . .

I am a professor of rhetoric," Chamberlain said. "I am fairly certain I have nothing you would care to learn. I am a teacher with a cause in my heart and men to lead. These poor men . . . their leader has no real knowledge of warfare or tactics. I am only a stubborn man, Ponder. That is my greatest advantage in this fight. I have deep within me the inability to do nothing. I may die today, but I will not die with a bullet in my back. I will not die in retreat. I am, at least, like the apostle Paul, who wrote, 'This one thing I do . . . I press toward the mark.'"

I have read the third decision for success today.   ☐ A.M.   ☐ P.M.

In applying this decision, today I would give myself a grade of: **A B C D**

I SEIZE THIS MOMENT. I CHOOSE NOW. I AM A PERSON OF ACTION.

What was your motivation in making that difficult
choice to do the honorable thing?

_____

_____

_____

_____

_____

_____

_____

_____

_____

_____

_____

_____

_____

_____

_____

_____

_____

_____

_____

I have read the third decision for success today.   ☐ A.M.   ☐ P.M.

In applying this decision, today I would give myself a grade of: **A B C D**

I SEIZE THIS MOMENT. I CHOOSE NOW. I AM A PERSON OF ACTION.

Between a rock and a hard place, the saying goes.
What is your first response when you find yourself there?
Are you a 'white flag waver'?

From *The Traveler's Gift* . . .

Deep in thought, Chamberlain was quickly sorting the situation. *We can't retreat.* he said to himself. *We can't stay here. When I am faced with the choice of doing nothing or doing something, I will always choose to act.*

I have read the third decision for success today.   ☐ A.M.   ☐ P.M.

In applying this decision, today I would give myself a grade of: **A B C D**

I SEIZE THIS MOMENT. I CHOOSE NOW. I AM A PERSON OF ACTION.

Do you analyze and strategize and hunker down for the plan to materialize? Or do you begin to fight your way out?

_____

_____

_____

_____

_____

_____

_____

_____

_____

_____

_____

_____

_____

_____

_____

_____

_____

_____

_____

I have read the third decision for success today.   ☐ A.M.   ☐ P.M.

In applying this decision, today I would give myself a grade of: **A B C D**

I SEIZE THIS MOMENT. I CHOOSE NOW. I AM A PERSON OF ACTION.

Merging in 70-mph, rush-hour traffic in any metropolitan city in the United States is an exercise not in patience but in acceleration. Knowing exactly when to swerve your way into the path of other daring drivers. Where would you get if you just decided to park the car instead?

From *The Traveler's Gift* . . .

M any people move out of the way for a person on the run; others are caught up in his wake.

I have read the third decision for success today.   ☐ A.M.   ☐ P.M.

In applying this decision, today I would give myself a grade of: **A B C D**

I SEIZE THIS MOMENT. I CHOOSE NOW. I AM A PERSON OF ACTION.

Do you often move out of the way for the person
on the run or get caught in the wake?
Are you ever that person on the run?

_____

_____

_____

_____

_____

_____

_____

_____

_____

_____

_____

_____

_____

_____

_____

_____

_____

_____

_____

_____

_____

I have read the third decision for success today.   ☐ A.M.   ☐ P.M.

In applying this decision, today I would give myself a grade of: **A B C D**

I SEIZE THIS MOMENT. I CHOOSE NOW. I AM A PERSON OF ACTION.

Imagine yourself in Chamberlain's shoes—an educated man, a teacher, with no military experience to fall back on. What caused him to keep going, despite the odds?

From *The Traveler's Gift* . . .

C hamberlain was standing in full view on the top of the wall, his arms crossed, staring down at the advancing enemy. . . . Turning his back to the Rebels, he looked down at his men. "Fix bayonets," he said.

I have read the third decision for success today.   ☐ A.M.   ☐ P.M.

In applying this decision, today I would give myself a grade of: **A B C D**

I SEIZE THIS MOMENT. I CHOOSE NOW. I AM A PERSON OF ACTION.

Do you strive to keep going despite the odds? What situation has caused you to face the odds and retreat?

_____

_____

_____

_____

_____

_____

_____

_____

_____

_____

_____

_____

_____

_____

_____

_____

_____

_____

_____

_____

_____

_____

I have read the third decision for success today. ☐ A.M. ☐ P.M.

In applying this decision, today I would give myself a grade of: **A B C D**

I SEIZE THIS MOMENT. I CHOOSE NOW. I AM A PERSON OF ACTION.

Is there anyone you would follow to the ends of the earth,
even if it meant certain death? What about that person
is worthy of such loyalty?

From *The Traveler's Gift* . . .

David watched in awe as Chamberlain drew his sword, leaped up onto the wall again, and screamed, "Bayonets! Bayonets!" Turning, the colonel pointed the sword directly at David and slightly bowed his head. Then he wheeled to face the overwhelming odds and slashed his blade through the air. With a power born of righteousness and fear, the schoolteacher from Maine roared, "Charge! Charge! Charge!" to his men, and they did.

I have read the third decision for success today.   ☐ A.M.   ☐ P.M.

In applying this decision, today I would give myself a grade of: **A B C D**

I SEIZE THIS MOMENT. I CHOOSE NOW. I AM A PERSON OF ACTION.

What leadership qualities do you possess
that sparks loyalty from others?

_____

_____

_____

_____

_____

_____

_____

_____

_____

_____

_____

_____

_____

_____

_____

_____

_____

_____

_____

_____

I have read the third decision for success today.   ☐ A.M.   ☐ P.M.

In applying this decision, today I would give myself a grade of: **A B C D**

I SEIZE THIS MOMENT. I CHOOSE NOW. I AM A PERSON OF ACTION.

Nothing is impossible with God, the Scriptures say, but that word 'with' is often overlooked. 'With' implies that you are a valuable a part of the equation. Sure, God can do the seemingly impossible with or without you. But he'd rather do it with, and through you. Are you ready to take action?

From *The Traveler's Gift* . . .

An army of sheep led by a lion would defeat an army of lions led by a sheep!

_____

_____

_____

_____

_____

_____

_____

_____

_____

_____

_____

_____

_____

_____

_____

_____

_____

_____

I have read the third decision for success today.   ☐ A.M.   ☐ P.M.

In applying this decision, today I would give myself a grade of: **A B C D**

I SEIZE THIS MOMENT. I CHOOSE NOW. I AM A PERSON OF ACTION.

What decisions have been made
in the past knowing God is with you?

_____

_____

_____

_____

_____

_____

_____

_____

_____

_____

_____

_____

_____

_____

_____

_____

_____

_____

_____

_____

_____

_____

I have read the third decision for success today.   ☐ A.M.   ☐ P.M.

In applying this decision, today I would give myself a grade of: **A B C D**

I SEIZE THIS MOMENT. I CHOOSE NOW. I AM A PERSON OF ACTION.

Could it be that while you're waiting for the future to happen,
God is waiting for you to step out in faith?

From *The Traveler's Gift* . . .

When faced with a decision, many people say they are waiting for God. But I understand, in most cases, God is waiting for me.

I have read the third decision for success today.   ☐ A.M.   ☐ P.M.

In applying this decision, today I would give myself a grade of: **A B C D**

I SEIZE THIS MOMENT. I CHOOSE NOW. I AM A PERSON OF ACTION.

Imagine what might that step of faith looks like. Is doesn't have to be a giant leap, just a movement. Are you moving forward? What is holding you back?

_____
_____
_____
_____
_____
_____
_____
_____
_____
_____
_____
_____
_____
_____
_____
_____
_____
_____
_____
_____
_____
_____

I have read the third decision for success today.   ☐ A.M.   ☐ P.M.

In applying this decision, today I would give myself a grade of: **A B C D**

I SEIZE THIS MOMENT. I CHOOSE NOW. I AM A PERSON OF ACTION.

Some people are naturally quick on their feet, quick on the draw. Whether quick or snail-slow, when was the last time you had to make a decision in a single moment. Was it a decision made quickly or slowly?

From *The Traveler's Gift* . . .

S uccessful people make their decisions quickly and change their minds slowly. Failures make their decisions slowly and change their minds quickly.

I have read the third decision for success today.   ☐ A.M.   ☐ P.M.

In applying this decision, today I would give myself a grade of: **A B C D**

I SEIZE THIS MOMENT. I CHOOSE NOW. I AM A PERSON OF ACTION.

Did that decision made in a single moment work out in the end?

I have read the third decision for success today. ☐ A.M. ☐ P.M.

In applying this decision, today I would give myself a grade of: **A B C D**

I SEIZE THIS MOMENT. I CHOOSE NOW. I AM A PERSON OF ACTION.

Write down what you fear the most. Now, suspend that thought just for a few minutes, and imagine what you could accomplish if that fear didn't exist. Where would you be, and what would you be doing with your life?

From *The Traveler's Gift* . . .

F ear no longer has a
    place in my life. For too
long, fear has outweighed
my desire to make things
better for my family. Never
again! I have exposed fear
as a vapor, an imposter that
never had any power over
me in the first place!

I have read the third decision for success today.   ☐ A.M.   ☐ P.M.

In applying this decision, today I would give myself a grade of: **A B C D**

I SEIZE THIS MOMENT. I CHOOSE NOW. I AM A PERSON OF ACTION.

What significant fears have you already overcome in life?

_____

_____

_____

_____

_____

_____

_____

_____

_____

_____

_____

_____

_____

_____

_____

_____

_____

_____

_____

_____

_____

_____

I have read the third decision for success today.   ☐ A.M.   ☐ P.M.

In applying this decision, today I would give myself a grade of: **A B C D**

I seize this moment. I choose now. I am a person of action.

Be still for just a moment and listen to the opinions of others that you have allowed to fester in your mind. Now press the 'mute' button. Make that the last minute you waste wallowing in what they think. What opinions of others do you need to erase from your memory?

From *The Traveler's Gift* . . .

I do not fear opinion, gossip, or the idle chatter of monkeys, for all are the same to me. I do not fear failure, for in my life, failure is a myth. Failure exists only for the person who quits.

_____
_____
_____
_____
_____
_____
_____
_____
_____
_____
_____
_____
_____
_____
_____
_____
_____

I have read the third decision for success today.   ☐ A.M.   ☐ P.M.

In applying this decision, today I would give myself a grade of: **A B C D**

I SEIZE THIS MOMENT. I CHOOSE NOW. I AM A PERSON OF ACTION.

What matters is what you believe about yourself.
What honest opinion do you have of yourself?

_____

_____

_____

_____

_____

_____

_____

_____

_____

_____

_____

_____

_____

_____

_____

_____

_____

_____

_____

_____

_____

_____

I have read the third decision for success today.   ☐ A.M.   ☐ P.M.

In applying this decision, today I would give myself a grade of: **A B C D**

I SEIZE THIS MOMENT. I CHOOSE NOW. I AM A PERSON OF ACTION.

"Great deeds are usually wrought at great risk," Herodotus, the Greek researcher and storyteller once said. What are you willing to risk in order to pursue your dream?

From *The Traveler's Gift* . . .

A bout seventy yards down the slope, David caught sight of Chamberlain. He had his left hand on the trunk of a tree, and in his right he held the sword, the point of which was resting on the collarbone of a Rebel soldier. The man had his hands up. It was over.

I have read the third decision for success today.   ☐ A.M.   ☐ P.M.

In applying this decision, today I would give myself a grade of: **A B C D**

I SEIZE THIS MOMENT. I CHOOSE NOW. I AM A PERSON OF ACTION.

The Active Decision
"I Am a Person of Action"
Write this decision in your own words.

_____

_____

_____

_____

_____

_____

_____

_____

_____

_____

_____

_____

_____

_____

_____

_____

_____

_____

_____

I have read the third decision for success today. ☐ A.M. ☐ P.M.

In applying this decision, today I would give myself a grade of: **A B C D**

I SEIZE THIS MOMENT. I CHOOSE NOW. I AM A PERSON OF ACTION.

Now express how this decision will change your life.

_____

_____

_____

_____

_____

_____

_____

_____

_____

_____

_____

_____

_____

_____

_____

_____

_____

_____

_____

_____

_____

_____

_____

_____

I have read the third decision for success today.   ☐ A.M.   ☐ P.M.

In applying this decision, today I would give myself a grade of: **A B C D**

The Certain Decision for Success

I Have a Decided Heart.

A wise man once said, "A journey of a thousand miles begins with a single step." Knowing this to be true, I am taking my first step today. For too long my feet have been tentative, shuffling left and right, more backward than forward as my heart gauged the direction of the wind. Criticism, condemnation, and complaint are creatures of the wind. They come and go on the wasted breath of lesser beings and have no power over me. The power to control direction belongs to me. Today I will begin to exercise that power. My course has been charted. My destiny is assured.

I have a decided heart. I am passionate about my vision for the future. I will awaken every morning with an excitement about the new day and its opportunity for growth and change. My thoughts and actions will work in a forward motion, never sliding into the dark forest of doubt or the muddy quicksand of self-pity. I will freely give my vision for the future to others, and as they see the belief in my eyes, they will follow me.

I will lay my head on my pillow at night happily exhausted, knowing that I have done everything within my power to move the mountains in my path. As I sleep, the same dream that dominates my waking hours will be with me in the dark. Yes, I have a dream. It is a great dream, and I will never apologize for it. Neither will I ever let it go, for if I did, my life would be finished. My hopes, my passions, my vision for the future are my very existence. A person without a dream never had a dream come true.

I have a decided heart. I will not wait. I know that the purpose of analysis is to come to a conclusion. I have tested the angles. I have measured the probabilities. And now I have made a decision with my heart. I am not timid. I will move now and not look back. What I put off until tomorrow, I will put off until the next day as well. I do not procrastinate. All my problems become smaller when I confront them. If I touch a thistle with caution, it will prick me, but if I grasp it boldly, its spines crumble into dust.

I will not wait.

I am passionate about my vision for the future.

My course has been charted.

My destiny is assured.

I have a decided heart.

MY DESTINY IS ASSURED. I HAVE A DECIDED HEART.

Think about the future in terms of adventure. What adventure are you going on? Do you know where you are going?

From *The Traveler's Gift* . . .

"Do you know where you are?" is a question that affects me not in the least!" Colon said, [shaking] his head in disgust. Now, "Do you know where you are going?"—there is a question I can answer!"

I have read the fourth decision for success today.   ☐ A.M.   ☐ P.M.

In applying this decision, today I would give myself a grade of: **A B C D**

MY DESTINY IS ASSURED. I HAVE A DECIDED HEART.

What possibilities hold the most excitement,
and hold the most uncertainty?

_____

_____

_____

_____

_____

_____

_____

_____

_____

_____

_____

_____

_____

_____

_____

_____

_____

_____

_____

_____

_____

_____

I have read the fourth decision for success today.   ☐ A.M.   ☐ P.M.

In applying this decision, today I would give myself a grade of: **A B C D**

MY DESTINY IS ASSURED. I HAVE A DECIDED HEART.

Write down one big lie, one socially acceptable 'truth' that most people swallow hook, line and sinker. Do you believe it? Have you ever believed it?

From *The Traveler's Gift* . . .

Truth is truth. If a thousand people believe something foolish, it is still foolish! Truth is never dependent upon consensus of opinion. I have found that it is better to be alone and acting upon the truth in my heart than to follow a gaggle of silly geese doomed to mediocrity.

I have read the fourth decision for success today.   ☐ A.M.   ☐ P.M.

In applying this decision, today I would give myself a grade of: **A B C D**

My destiny is assured. I have a decided heart.

What truth do you see as something rejected by most of society?
What consequences do they face for ignoring that truth?

_____

_____

_____

_____

_____

_____

_____

_____

_____

_____

_____

_____

_____

_____

_____

_____

_____

_____

_____

_____

I have read the fourth decision for success today. ☐ A.M. ☐ P.M.

In applying this decision, today I would give myself a grade of: **A B C D**

MY DESTINY IS ASSURED. I HAVE A DECIDED HEART.

"Keeping up with the Jones" has killed its share of decent men and women. But the Joneses only kept to themselves. Who are the Joneses in your life, and why do they matter?

From *The Traveler's Gift* . . .

I f you worry about what other people think of you, then you will have more confidence in their opinion than you have in your own. Poor is the man whose future depends on the opinions and permission of others. Remember this, if you are afraid of criticism, you will die doing nothing!

I have read the fourth decision for success today.   ☐ A.M.   ☐ P.M.

In applying this decision, today I would give myself a grade of: **A B C D**

My destiny is assured. I have a decided heart.

Are you a person of passion? If asked to show proof, what evidence would you give?

From *The Traveler's Gift* . . .

G etting started, getting finished—both ends of a journey require a demonstration of passion.

I have read the fourth decision for success today.   ☐ A.M.   ☐ P.M.

In applying this decision, today I would give myself a grade of: **A B C D**

MY DESTINY IS ASSURED. I HAVE A DECIDED HEART.

Has criticism from others every stifled your passion? Do you allow it to hinder your moving forward?

_____

_____

_____

_____

_____

_____

_____

_____

_____

_____

_____

_____

_____

_____

_____

_____

_____

_____

I have read the fourth decision for success today.   ☐ A.M.   ☐ P.M.

In applying this decision, today I would give myself a grade of: **A B C D**

My destiny is assured. I have a decided heart.

*Columbus endured public humiliation and ridicule for 19 years—
all for his convictions, what he knew to be true. Is there anything
about which you feel that strongly?*

From *The Traveler's Gift* . . .

C olumbus grabbed
David by the
shoulders and shook him
once as he said, "My friend!
The world is a sphere! It is
not flat! We are sailing
around the earth on the
smooth surface of a sphere.
We will not fall off some
imaginary edge!"

"Are you the only person
who believes this?" David
asked.

"At the moment, yes."
Columbus said, "but that
bothers me not in the least."

I have read the fourth decision for success today.   ☐ A.M.   ☐ P.M.

In applying this decision, today I would give myself a grade of: **A B C D**

MY DESTINY IS ASSURED. I HAVE A DECIDED HEART.

*What convictions need to be added to
your life in order to build character?*

_____

_____

_____

_____

_____

_____

_____

_____

_____

_____

_____

_____

_____

_____

_____

_____

_____

_____

_____

_____

I have read the fourth decision for success today.   ☐ A.M.   ☐ P.M.

In applying this decision, today I would give myself a grade of: **A B C D**

MY DESTINY IS ASSURED. I HAVE A DECIDED HEART.

Write out your life-long dream—that ultimate accomplishment or desire you've set your heart on.

From *The Traveler's Gift* . . .

P assion is a product of the heart. Passion is what helps you when you have a great dream. Passion breeds conviction and turns mediocrity into excellence! Your passion will motivate others to join you in pursuit of your dream. With passion, you will overcome insurmountable obstacles. You will become unstoppable!

I have read the fourth decision for success today.   ☐ A.M.   ☐ P.M.

In applying this decision, today I would give myself a grade of: **A B C D**

My destiny is assured. I have a decided heart.

Now take that dream and build an even more
fantastic sequel to it. What does that look like?

_____

_____

_____

_____

_____

_____

_____

_____

_____

_____

_____

_____

_____

_____

_____

_____

_____

_____

_____

_____

I have read the fourth decision for success today.   ☐ A.M.   ☐ P.M.

In applying this decision, today I would give myself a grade of: **A B C D**

MY DESTINY IS ASSURED. I HAVE A DECIDED HEART.

On a scale of 1 to 5, how much of a realist are you? What does
the realist say to you to try to squash your dream?

From *The Traveler's Gift* . . .

N othing great was ever
accomplished by a
realistic person!

_____

_____

_____

_____

_____

_____

_____

_____

_____

_____

_____

_____

_____

_____

_____

_____

_____

_____

_____

I have read the fourth decision for success today.   ☐ A.M.   ☐ P.M.

In applying this decision, today I would give myself a grade of: **A B C D**

MY DESTINY IS ASSURED. I HAVE A DECIDED HEART.

Imagine you're a contestant on "Let's Make A Deal" (remember that game show from the '60s and '70s?), and the lovely Carol Merrill invites you to choose between two curtains. On one, the word "Commitment." On the other, "Exit." Which one are you most likely to choose today? And why?

From *The Traveler's Gift* . . .

M ost people fail at whatever they attempt because of an undecided heart. Should I? Should I not? Go forward? Go back? Success requires the emotional balance of a committed heart. When confronted with a challenge, the committed heart will search for a solution. The undecided heart searches for escape.

I have read the fourth decision for success today.   ☐ A.M.   ☐ P.M.

In applying this decision, today I would give myself a grade of: **A B C D**

MY DESTINY IS ASSURED. I HAVE A DECIDED HEART.

Have you ever overcome the temptation to have an
undecided heart? What will help you gain the emotional
balance of a committed heart?

_____

_____

_____

_____

_____

_____

_____

_____

_____

_____

_____

_____

_____

_____

_____

_____

_____

_____

_____

I have read the fourth decision for success today.   ☐ A.M.   ☐ P.M.

In applying this decision, today I would give myself a grade of: **A B C D**

MY DESTINY IS ASSURED. I HAVE A DECIDED HEART.

What do you think Columbus meant when
he said 'I have a decided heart'?

From *The Traveler's Gift* . . .

David took the yellowed paper, glanced at it briefly and said, "You will find your new world."

Columbus, eyes still straight ahead, spoke quietly. 'I know."

David smiled and shook his head in wonder. "How do you know?" he asked.

Columbus turned and looked at David. "I have a decided heart," he said and turned back.

_____

I have read the fourth decision for success today.   ☐ A.M.   ☐ P.M.

In applying this decision, today I would give myself a grade of: **A B C D**

MY DESTINY IS ASSURED. I HAVE A DECIDED HEART.

The right time is right now. What can you do this very day to move one step closer to where you want to be?

From *The Traveler's Gift* . . .

A committed heart does not wait for conditions to be exactly right. Why? Because conditions are never exactly right. Indecision limits the Almighty and his ability to perform miracles in your life. He has put the vision in you—proceed! To wait, to wonder, to doubt, to be indecisive is to disobey God.

I have read the fourth decision for success today.   ☐ A.M.   ☐ P.M.

In applying this decision, today I would give myself a grade of: **A B C D**

Reflect on a time when you were committed even though conditions did not seem right. What was the end result?

_____

_____

_____

_____

_____

_____

_____

_____

_____

_____

_____

_____

_____

_____

_____

_____

_____

_____

_____

_____

_____

I have read the fourth decision for success today.   ☐ A.M.   ☐ P.M.

In applying this decision, today I would give myself a grade of: **A B C D**

MY DESTINY IS ASSURED. I HAVE A DECIDED HEART.

Without thinking too hard, write down three positive facts you know about yourself. Once you write them, go back and answer 'How?' for each fact.

From *The Traveler's Gift* . . .

C riticism, condemnation, and complaint are creatures of the wind. They come and go on the wasted breath of lesser beings and have no power over me.

_____

_____

_____

_____

_____

_____

_____

_____

_____

_____

_____

_____

_____

_____

_____

_____

_____

_____

_____

I have read the fourth decision for success today.   ☐ A.M.   ☐ P.M.

In applying this decision, today I would give myself a grade of: **A B C D**

MY DESTINY IS ASSURED. I HAVE A DECIDED HEART.

What was your mother's dream? Your father's? Did they ever tell you, or did their dreams take a back seat to the necessities of life? If you could go back and talk to them when they were your age, when their dreams were still possible, what would you say to them?

From *The Traveler's Gift* . . .

A person without a dream never had a dream come true.

I have read the fourth decision for success today.   ☐ A.M.   ☐ P.M.

In applying this decision, today I would give myself a grade of: **A B C D**

MY DESTINY IS ASSURED. I HAVE A DECIDED HEART.

When it comes to making decisions,
which of the following describes you best and why?
"Ready, Aim, Aim, Aim . . ."
"Set, Set, Set, Almost Ready, [hesitant] Fire" or
'Fire! Fire, uh, . . . oops."

From *The Traveler's Gift* . . .

I know the purpose of analysis is to come to a conclusion. I have tested the angles. I have measured the probabilities. And now I have made a decision with my heart.

I have read the fourth decision for success today.   ☐ A.M.   ☐ P.M.

In applying this decision, today I would give myself a grade of: **A B C D**

Some people see any kind of confrontation as something to avoid. But it's been said that we only really think when we confront a problem. Have you given real thought to a problem lately? Did you find a solution?

From *The Traveler's Gift* . . .

All my problems become smaller when I confront them. If I touch a thistle with caution, it will prick me, but if I grasp it boldly, its spines crumble into dust.

I have read the fourth decision for success today.   ☐ A.M.   ☐ P.M.

In applying this decision, today I would give myself a grade of: **A B C D**

My destiny is assured. I have a decided heart.

The Certain Decision
"I Have a Decided Heart"
Write this decision in your own words.

_____

_____

_____

_____

_____

_____

_____

_____

_____

_____

_____

_____

_____

_____

_____

_____

_____

_____

_____

I have read the fourth decision for success today.   ☐ A.M.   ☐ P.M.

In applying this decision, today I would give myself a grade of: **A B C D**

MY DESTINY IS ASSURED. I HAVE A DECIDED HEART.

Now express how this decision will change your life.

_____

_____

_____

_____

_____

_____

_____

_____

_____

_____

_____

_____

_____

_____

_____

_____

_____

_____

I have read the fourth decision for success today. ☐ A.M. ☐ P.M.

In applying this decision, today I would give myself a grade of: **A B C D**

The Joyful Decision for Success

TODAY, I CHOOSE TO BE HAPPY.

Beginning this very moment, I am a happy person, for I now truly understand the concept of happiness. Few others before me have been able to grasp the truth of the physical law that enables one to live happily every day. I know now that happiness is not an emotional phantom floating in and out of my life. Happiness is a choice. Happiness is the end result of certain thoughts and activities, which actually bring about a chemical reaction in my body. This reaction results in a euphoria that, while elusive to some, is totally under my control.

Today I will choose to be happy. I will greet each day with laughter. Within moments of awakening, I will laugh for seven seconds. Even after such a small period of time, excitement has begun to flow through my bloodstream. I feel different. I am different! I am enthusiastic about the day. I am alert to its possibilities. I am happy! Laughter is an outward expression of enthusiasm, and I know that enthusiasm is the fuel that moves the world. I laugh throughout the day. I laugh while I am alone, and I laugh in conversation with others. People are drawn to me because I have laughter in my heart. The world belongs to the enthusiastic, for people will follow them anywhere!

Today I will choose to be happy. I will smile at every person I meet. My smile has become my calling card. It is, after all, the most potent weapon I possess. My smile has the strength to forge bonds, break ice, and calm storms. I will use my smile constantly. Because of my smile, the people with whom I come in contact on a daily basis will choose to further my causes and follow my leadership. I will always smile first. That particular display of a good attitude will tell others what I expect in return. My smile is the key to my emotional makeup. A wise man once said, "I do not sing because I am happy; I am happy because I sing!" When I choose to smile, I become the master of my emotions. Discouragement, despair, frustration, and fear will always wither when confronted by my smile. The power of who I am is displayed when I smile.

Today I will choose to be happy. I am the possessor of a grateful spirit. In the past, I have found discouragement in particular situations until I compared the condition of my life to others less fortunate. Just as a fresh breeze cleans smoke from the air, so a grateful spirit removes the cloud of despair. It is impossible for the seeds of depression to take root in a thankful heart. My God has bestowed upon me many gifts, and for these I will remember to be grateful. Too many times I have offered up the prayers of a beggar, always asking for more and forgetting to give thanks. I do not wish to be seen as a greedy child, unappreciative and disrespectful. I am grateful for sight and sound and breath. If ever in my life there is a pouring out of blessings beyond that, then I will be grateful for the miracle of abundance.

I will greet each day with laughter.

I will smile at every person I meet.

I am the possessor of a grateful spirit.

Today I will choose to be happy.

TODAY I WILL CHOOSE TO BE HAPPY. I AM THE POSSESSOR OF A GRATEFUL SPIRIT.

Wisdom according to Ziggy: "You can complain because roses have thorns, or you can rejoice because thorns have roses." (No wonder his cartoon head was so big.) Be honest. Do you choose to complain more often than not? What do you complain most about?

From *The Traveler's Gift* . . .

I do not complain," Anne said. "Papa says complaining is an activity just as jumping rope or listening to the radio is an activity. One may choose to turn on the radio, and one may choose not to turn on the radio. One may choose to complain, and one may choose not to complain. I choose not to complain."

I have read the fifth decision for success today.   ☐ A.M.   ☐ P.M.

In applying this decision, today I would give myself a grade of: **A B C D**

TODAY I WILL CHOOSE TO BE HAPPY. I AM THE POSSESSOR OF A GRATEFUL SPIRIT.

Continue to be very honest. Are you willing to work on not complaining as often? Make a list of things that will no longer be complaints?

I have read the fifth decision for success today.   ☐ A.M.   ☐ P.M.

In applying this decision, today I would give myself a grade of: **A B C D**

TODAY I WILL CHOOSE TO BE HAPPY. I AM THE POSSESSOR OF A GRATEFUL SPIRIT.

What significant choices, good and bad, have fashioned your life the most?

From *The Traveler's Gift* . . .

A nne tilted her head to the side as if she were having difficulty understanding. Sweeping a lock of hair from her eyes, she said patiently, "Our very lives are fashioned by choice, Mr. Ponder. First we make choices. Then our choices make us."

I have read the fifth decision for success today.   ☐ A.M.   ☐ P.M.

In applying this decision, today I would give myself a grade of: **A B C D**

TODAY I WILL CHOOSE TO BE HAPPY. I AM THE POSSESSOR OF A GRATEFUL SPIRIT.

The loaded nature of the question aside,
what have your choices made of you?

_____

_____

_____

_____

_____

_____

_____

_____

_____

_____

_____

_____

_____

_____

_____

_____

_____

_____

_____

I have read the fifth decision for success today.   ☐ A.M.   ☐ P.M.

In applying this decision, today I would give myself a grade of: **A B C D**

TODAY I WILL CHOOSE TO BE HAPPY. I AM THE POSSESSOR OF A GRATEFUL SPIRIT.

"My mother's menu consisted of two choices," comedian Buddy Hackett said. "Take it or leave it." When your feet first hit the floor this morning, what choice did you make?

From *The Traveler's Gift* . . .

If I ever find myself in a bad mood, I immediately make a choice to be happy," said Anne. "In fact, it is the first choice I make every day. I say out loud to my mirror, 'Today, I will choose to be happy!' I smile into the mirror and laugh even if I am sad. I just say, 'Ha, ha, ha, ha!' And soon, I am happy, exactly as I have chosen to be."

I have read the fifth decision for success today.   ☐ A.M.   ☐ P.M.

In applying this decision, today I would give myself a grade of: **A B C D**

TODAY I WILL CHOOSE TO BE HAPPY. I AM THE POSSESSOR OF A GRATEFUL SPIRIT.

What helps you make the choice to be happy?
What type of day makes it more difficult?

_____

_____

_____

_____

_____

_____

_____

_____

_____

_____

_____

_____

_____

_____

_____

_____

_____

_____

_____

I have read the fifth decision for success today. ☐ A.M. ☐ P.M.

In applying this decision, today I would give myself a grade of: **A B C D**

Take a fictional character that stands out in your memory, your most vocal co-worker, and the person whose advice you seek most often. Stand them up like toy soldiers in your hand. Who would they be? What are they likely to talk about?

From *The Traveler's Gift* . . .

M y life—my
personality, my
habits, even my speech—is
a combination of the books
I choose to read, the people
I choose to listen to, and
the thoughts I choose to
tolerate in my mind.

I have read the fifth decision for success today.   ☐ A.M.   ☐ P.M.

In applying this decision, today I would give myself a grade of: **A B C D**

TODAY I WILL CHOOSE TO BE HAPPY. I AM THE POSSESSOR OF A GRATEFUL SPIRIT.

*Back to the toy soldiers, why would their
conversation be worth hearing?*

_____

_____

_____

_____

_____

_____

_____

_____

_____

_____

_____

_____

_____

_____

_____

_____

_____

_____

_____

_____

_____

_____

I have read the fifth decision for success today. ☐ A.M. ☐ P.M.

In applying this decision, today I would give myself a grade of: A B C D

What's inside makes the difference between ordinary and extraordinary. And you get to choose what goes inside! List five qualities you already possess that make you proud.

From *The Traveler's Gift* . . .

I tugged on Papa's arm and asked, 'Papa, which color balloon will go the highest?' And he said to me, 'Anne, it's not the color of the balloon that is important. It's what's inside that makes all the difference.'"

Then she looked David directly in the eye and said, "Mr. Ponder, I don't believe that being Jewish or Aryan or African has any bearing on what one can become. Greatness does not care if one is a girl or a boy. If, in fact, it is what's inside us that makes all the difference, then the difference is made when we choose what goes inside."

I have read the fifth decision for success today.   ☐ A.M.   ☐ P.M.

In applying this decision, today I would give myself a grade of: **A B C D**

TODAY I WILL CHOOSE TO BE HAPPY. I AM THE POSSESSOR OF A GRATEFUL SPIRIT.

Now list five more qualities of your choosing. It's your choice!
What steps will you take to gain those qualities?

_____

_____

_____

_____

_____

_____

_____

_____

_____

_____

_____

_____

_____

_____

_____

_____

_____

_____

_____

_____

_____

I have read the fifth decision for success today.   ☐ A.M.   ☐ P.M.

In applying this decision, today I would give myself a grade of: **A B C D**

TODAY I WILL CHOOSE TO BE HAPPY. I AM THE POSSESSOR OF A GRATEFUL SPIRIT.

If the ocean were like a bathtub with one big stopper holding all the water in, would you choose to drain the ocean with a teaspoon anyway or take a deep breath and dive in to try and pull the stopper?

From *The Traveler's Gift* . . .

David could feel the pulse pounding in his head. "I think that she probably would be afraid, Anne. Are you?"

Anne pulled her hand down from the rose and clasped both hands in front of her. Momentarily, she cut her eyes toward David, then back to the pictures. "Sometimes," she said. "But most often, I choose not to be. Papa says, 'Fear is a poor chisel with which to carve out tomorrow.'"

I have read the fifth decision for success today.   ☐ A.M.   ☐ P.M.

In applying this decision, today I would give myself a grade of: **A B C D**

TODAY I WILL CHOOSE TO BE HAPPY. I AM THE POSSESSOR OF A GRATEFUL SPIRIT.

When did you let fear carve out a day that you regret?
Are you striving to let go of fear when facing tomorrow?

_____

_____

_____

_____

_____

_____

_____

_____

_____

_____

_____

_____

_____

_____

_____

_____

_____

_____

_____

_____

I have read the fifth decision for success today.   ☐ A.M.   ☐ P.M.

In applying this decision, today I would give myself a grade of: **A B C D**

TODAY I WILL CHOOSE TO BE HAPPY. I AM THE POSSESSOR OF A GRATEFUL SPIRIT.

In the grand scheme of things, a Pollyanna outlook—a positive, "come what may I'll be okay" perspective—isn't the worst approach to life. Is there a Pollyanna in you?

From *The Traveler's Gift* . . .

Anne turned and faced David. "I will have a tomorrow, Mr. Ponder. Margot and Mrs. Petronella, they make fun of me. They call me a Pollyanna. They say that I live in a dream world, that I do not face reality. This is not true. I know that the war is horrible. I understand that we are in terrible danger here. I do not deny the reality of our situation. I deny the finality of it. This, too, shall pass."

I have read the fifth decision for success today. ☐ A.M. ☐ P.M.

In applying this decision, today I would give myself a grade of: **A B C D**

TODAY I WILL CHOOSE TO BE HAPPY. I AM THE POSSESSOR OF A GRATEFUL SPIRIT.

Who is the Pollyanna in your circle of friends?
What do you gain most from that relationship?

_____

_____

_____

_____

_____

_____

_____

_____

_____

_____

_____

_____

_____

_____

_____

_____

_____

_____

_____

_____

_____

_____

I have read the fifth decision for success today.   ☐ A.M.   ☐ P.M.

In applying this decision, today I would give myself a grade of: **A B C D**

TODAY I WILL CHOOSE TO BE HAPPY. I AM THE POSSESSOR OF A GRATEFUL SPIRIT.

Name a person that you are convinced is living life to the fullest. What makes them live that way?

From *The Traveler's Gift* . . .

Anne paused again. "I must go eat," she said. "You will be gone when I return?"
"Yes."
"Then remember me," Anne said, smiling. "I will remember you. But most of all, both of us must remember that life itself is a privilege, but to live life to its fullest—well, that is a choice!"

I have read the fifth decision for success today. ☐ A.M. ☐ P.M.

In applying this decision, today I would give myself a grade of: **A B C D**

TODAY I WILL CHOOSE TO BE HAPPY. I AM THE POSSESSOR OF A GRATEFUL SPIRIT.

What is your simplest pleasure, one small thing that always makes you happy?

From *The Traveler's Gift* . . .

H appiness is a choice. Happiness is the end result of certain thoughts and activities, which actually bring about a chemical reaction in my body. This reaction results in a euphoria that, while elusive to some, is totally under my control.

I have read the fifth decision for success today. ☐ A.M. ☐ P.M.

In applying this decision, today I would give myself a grade of: **A B C D**

TODAY I WILL CHOOSE TO BE HAPPY. I AM THE POSSESSOR OF A GRATEFUL SPIRIT.

Henry David Thoreau once wrote, "None are so old as those who have outlived enthusiasm." Eager to grow old? Me neither. Is your heart full of laughter?

From *The Traveler's Gift* . . .

People are drawn to me because I have laughter in my heart. The world belongs to the enthusiastic, for people will follow them anywhere!

I have read the fifth decision for success today.   ☐ A.M.   ☐ P.M.

In applying this decision, today I would give myself a grade of: **A B C D**

TODAY I WILL CHOOSE TO BE HAPPY. I AM THE POSSESSOR OF A GRATEFUL SPIRIT.

What brings enthusiasm to your life?
Are people drawn to your enthusiasm or is it too often hidden?

I have read the fifth decision for success today. ☐ A.M. ☐ P.M.

In applying this decision, today I would give myself a grade of: **A B C D**

TODAY I WILL CHOOSE TO BE HAPPY. I AM THE POSSESSOR OF A GRATEFUL SPIRIT.

Who would've thought that survival and success could depend on your ability to smile and mean it? Would you?

From *The Traveler's Gift* . . .

M y smile has become my calling card. It is, after all, the most potent weapon I possess. My smile has the strength to forge bonds, break ice, and calm storms. I will use my smile constantly. Because of my smile, the people with whom I come in contact on a daily basis will choose to further my causes and follow my leadership. I will always smile first. That particular display of a good attitude will tell others what I expect in return.

I have read the fifth decision for success today.   ☐ A.M.   ☐ P.M.

In applying this decision, today I would give myself a grade of: **A B C D**

Your smile is powerful. It says to the world, "Life is good! Count the number of times you remember smiling (on purpose) today. What were you communicating at the time?

From *The Traveler's Gift* . . .

When I choose to smile, I become the master of my emotions. Discouragement, despair, frustration, and fear will always wither when confronted by my smile. The power of who I am is displayed when I smile.

I have read the fifth decision for success today. ☐ A.M. ☐ P.M.

In applying this decision, today I would give myself a grade of: **A B C D**

Today I will choose to be happy. I am the possessor of a grateful spirit.

Quick! Make a short list of the things and people you simply wouldn't want to live without. Say each name or possession or thing aloud and be thankful for each gift.

From *The Traveler's Gift* . . .

In the past, I have found discouragement in particular situations until I compared the condition of my life to others less fortunate. Just as a fresh breeze cleans smoke from the air, so a grateful spirit removes the cloud of despair. It is impossible for the seeds of depression to take root in a thankful heart.

I have read the fifth decision for success today.   ☐ A.M.   ☐ P.M.

In applying this decision, today I would give myself a grade of: **A B C D**

TODAY I WILL CHOOSE TO BE HAPPY. I AM THE POSSESSOR OF A GRATEFUL SPIRIT.

The Joyful Decision
"Today, I Choose to Be Happy"
Write this decision in your own words.

_____

_____

_____

_____

_____

_____

_____

_____

_____

_____

_____

_____

_____

_____

_____

_____

_____

_____

_____

I have read the fifth decision for success today. ☐ A.M. ☐ P.M.

In applying this decision, today I would give myself a grade of: **A B C D**

TODAY I WILL CHOOSE TO BE HAPPY. I AM THE POSSESSOR OF A GRATEFUL SPIRIT.

Now express how this decision will change your life.

_____

_____

_____

_____

_____

_____

_____

_____

_____

_____

_____

_____

_____

_____

_____

_____

_____

_____

_____

_____

I have read the fifth decision for success today.   ☐ A.M.   ☐ P.M.

In applying this decision, today I would give myself a grade of: **A B C D**

The Compassionate Decision for Success

I WILL GREET THIS DAY WITH A FORGIVING SPIRIT.

For too long, every ounce of forgiveness I owned was locked away, hidden from view, waiting for me to bestow its precious presence upon some worthy person. Alas, I found most people to be singularly unworthy of my valuable forgiveness, and since they never asked for any, I kept it all for myself. Now, the forgiveness that I hoarded has sprouted inside my heart like a crippled seed yielding bitter fruit.

No more! At this moment, my life has taken on new hope and assurance. Of all the world's population, I am one of the few possessors of the secret to dissipating anger and resentment. I now understand that forgiveness has value only when it is given away. By the simple act of granting forgiveness, I release the demons of the past about which I can do nothing, and I create in myself a new heart, a new beginning.

I will greet this day with a forgiving spirit. I will forgive even those who do not ask for forgiveness. Many are the times when I have seethed in anger at a word or deed thrown into my life by an unthinking or uncaring person. I have wasted valuable hours imagining revenge or confrontation. Now I see the truth revealed about this psychological rock inside my shoe. The rage I nurture is often one-sided, for my offender seldom gives thought to his offense!

I will now and forevermore silently offer my forgiveness even to those who do not see that they need it. By the act of forgiving, I am no longer consumed by unproductive thoughts. I give up my bitterness. I am content in my soul and effective again with my fellowman. I will greet this day with a forgiving spirit. I will forgive those who criticize me unjustly.

Knowing that slavery in any form is wrong, I also know that the person who lives a life according to the opinion of others is a slave. I am not a slave. I have chosen my counsel. I know the difference between right and wrong. I know what is best for the future of my family, and neither misguided opinion nor unjust criticism will alter my course.

Those who are critical of my goals and dreams simply do not understand the higher purpose to which I have been called. Therefore, their scorn does not affect my attitude or action. I forgive their lack of vision, and I forge ahead. I now know that criticism is part of the price paid for leaping past mediocrity.

I will greet this day with a forgiving spirit. I will forgive myself. For many years, my greatest enemy has been myself. Every mistake, every miscalculation, every stumble I made has been replayed again and again in my mind. Every broken promise, every day wasted, every goal not reached has compounded the disgust I feel for the lack of achievement in my life. My dismay has developed a paralyzing grip. When I disappoint myself, I respond with inaction and become more disappointed.

I realize today that it is impossible to fight an enemy living in my head. By forgiving myself, I erase the doubts, fears, and frustration that have kept my past in the present. From this day forward, my history will cease to control my destiny. I have forgiven myself. My life has just begun.

I will forgive even those who do not ask for forgiveness.

I will forgive those who criticize me unjustly.

I will forgive myself.

I will greet this day with a forgiving spirit.

127

I WILL GREET THIS DAY WITH A FORGIVING SPIRIT. I WILL FORGIVE MYSELF.

Prayer and patience go hand in hand, but even if the answer isn't clear, the clearest path to peace begins with one step in the right direction. Is there something positive you can be doing while you're waiting for change?

From *The Traveler's Gift* . . .

L incoln let his fingers play softly across the large silk band. "This is a piece of cloth I carry with me in memory of Willie, my little boy. He died only a few months ago." He took a deep breath and sighed. "Now my son Tad has taken to bed . . . deathly ill. Mrs. Lincoln did not agree that I should be here today."

"Why did you come?"

"Duty. I knew I could choose to pray for my son while wandering about the White House. I am quite confident the Almighty hears my cry no matter the location. I also believe the good Lord would rather me pray and work, not pray and wait."

I have read the sixth decision for success today.   ☐ A.M.   ☐ P.M.

In applying this decision, today I would give myself a grade of: **A B C D**

I WILL GREET THIS DAY WITH A FORGIVING SPIRIT. I WILL FORGIVE MYSELF.

How do you view those searching for power?
What created their desire for power?

From *The Traveler's Gift* . . .

David tilted his head to the side. Confused, he said, "I'm lost here. In the first place, what does personal growth have to do with power? And in the second place, no offense, but I have no interest in power anyway."

Leaning forward, Lincoln said, "Mr. Ponder . . . David, if that is true, if you have no interest in power, then an incalculable amount of attention is being wasted on you. Some of it at this very moment!"

I have read the sixth decision for success today.   ☐ A.M.   ☐ P.M.

In applying this decision, today I would give myself a grade of: **A B C D**

I WILL GREET THIS DAY WITH A FORGIVING SPIRIT. I WILL FORGIVE MYSELF.

What interest do you have in power? In what areas of your life do you see personal growth leading to power?

_____

_____

_____

_____

_____

_____

_____

_____

_____

_____

_____

_____

_____

_____

_____

_____

_____

_____

_____

I have read the sixth decision for success today. ☐ A.M. ☐ P.M.

In applying this decision, today I would give myself a grade of: **A B C D**

I WILL GREET THIS DAY WITH A FORGIVING SPIRIT. I WILL FORGIVE MYSELF.

Some people think of the quest for power much like the love of money—the root of all evil. Do you agree that power is essential if we are to reach our personal potential? Why or why not?

From *The Traveler's Gift . . .*

P ersonal growth leads to power. There is a certain level of personal growth that will provide the skills necessary to feed and clothe one's family. There is another level of personal growth that will furnish influence and wisdom in sufficient quantities to be perceived a leader." Lincoln paused. He looked directly into the younger man's eyes. "But to do great deeds, great power is essential."

I have read the sixth decision for success today.   ☐ A.M.   ☐ P.M.

In applying this decision, today I would give myself a grade of: **A B C D**

I WILL GREET THIS DAY WITH A FORGIVING SPIRIT. I WILL FORGIVE MYSELF.

Think back to when you really thought you could make a difference in the world. How did you plan to do it? When did you begin to believe that was no longer possible?

From *The Traveler's Gift* . . .

Y ou see, some people want just enough power to get by," he said. "Then there are other people who will acquire enough power to make things more comfortable for their families, and they'll include other less fortunate souls in their charity if the personal growth part of the equation doesn't become too uncomfortable. But there are a few of us, David, who have latched on to this silly idea that we can change the world. We will develop the power to ignore what is popular and do what is right. One person can attain the power to lead hundreds of thousands of people to the promised land of their dreams."

I have read the sixth decision for success today. ☐ A.M. ☐ P.M.

In applying this decision, today I would give myself a grade of: **A B C D**

I WILL GREET THIS DAY WITH A FORGIVING SPIRIT. I WILL FORGIVE MYSELF.

Would you say that you're easy and interesting to be around? How did you arrive at that conclusion?

From *The Traveler's Gift* . . .

Seriously, questions such as, 'How do other people see me?' and 'What don't they like?' can be quite revealing if answered honestly. When you become a person whom others want to be around, you will have become a person of influence.

I have read the sixth decision for success today.   ☐ A.M.   ☐ P.M.

In applying this decision, today I would give myself a grade of: **A B C D**

I WILL GREET THIS DAY WITH A FORGIVING SPIRIT. I WILL FORGIVE MYSELF.

Answer this: "If I were God, what would I think of me?"

From *The Traveler's Gift* . . .

B ut you will never please everyone, nor should pleasing everyone be your goal. For example, to seek the approval of someone who is lazy or jealous is to cast your pearls before swine. You will find that God rarely uses a person whose main concern is what others are thinking.

I have read the sixth decision for success today. ☐ A.M. ☐ P.M.

In applying this decision, today I would give myself a grade of: **A B C D**

I WILL GREET THIS DAY WITH A FORGIVING SPIRIT. I WILL FORGIVE MYSELF.

Is there someone whose opinions are always on the table? A wise man once said, "Those who never retract their opinions love themselves more than they love the truth." Remember that, and allow the truth to set you free . . . to be who you were created to be.

From *The Traveler's Gift* . . .

L incoln stood and
shoved his hands into
his pockets. "Sooner or
later, every man of
character will have that
character questioned. Every
man of honor and courage
will be faced with unjust
criticism, but never forget
that unjust criticism has no
impact whatsoever upon
the truth. And the only
sure way to avoid criticism
is to do nothing and be
nothing!"

I have read the sixth decision for success today.   ☐ A.M.   ☐ P.M.

In applying this decision, today I would give myself a grade of: **A B C D**

I WILL GREET THIS DAY WITH A FORGIVING SPIRIT. I WILL FORGIVE MYSELF.

How flexible are your opinions? Are some things wrong only some of the time? Give one example. Does it hold up to scrutiny?

From *The Traveler's Gift* . . .

W hile public opinion might sway back and forth, right and wrong do not," Lincoln said.

I have read the sixth decision for success today. ☐ A.M. ☐ P.M.

In applying this decision, today I would give myself a grade of: **A B C D**

I WILL GREET THIS DAY WITH A FORGIVING SPIRIT. I WILL FORGIVE MYSELF.

People commit all manner of atrocities in the name of God. Trouble is, God had nothing to do with it. The only side worth risking anything for is God's side. Write down the team requirements for being on God's side. [Hint: you'll find it in Micah 6 v.8]

From *The Traveler's Gift* . . .

So your question was, 'Do I believe that God is on our side?' To be quite honest, I haven't given that question very much attention. I am much more concerned with whether we are on God's side.

I have read the sixth decision for success today.   ☐ A.M.   ☐ P.M.

In applying this decision, today I would give myself a grade of: **A B C D**

I WILL GREET THIS DAY WITH A FORGIVING SPIRIT. I WILL FORGIVE MYSELF.

Who are the winners in your life, the people who jump in and help at a moment's notice, the ones who show up on moving day? Would they say the same about you?

From *The Traveler's Gift* . . .

I f you are determined to win, you will have to surround yourself with winners. Don't be discouraged by the people you might choose for your team who talk big but produce little . . ." said Lincoln. "Just keep putting them in the boat to see who wants to paddle as hard as I do."

I have read the sixth decision for success today. ☐ A.M. ☐ P.M.

In applying this decision, today I would give myself a grade of: **A B C D**

I WILL GREET THIS DAY WITH A FORGIVING SPIRIT. I WILL FORGIVE MYSELF.

Is there anything so terrible that you could never forgive the one
who did it? Are you capable of committing so terrible a crime?
How can you be sure?

From *The Traveler's Gift* . . .

T he secret of
forgiveness," Lincoln
responded. "It is a secret
that is hidden in plain
sight. It costs nothing and is
worth millions. It is
available to everyone and
used by few. If you harness
the power of forgiveness,
you will be revered, sought
after, and wealthy. And not
coincidentally, you will also
be forgiven by others!"

I have read the sixth decision for success today.   ☐ A.M.   ☐ P.M.

In applying this decision, today I would give myself a grade of: **A B C D**

I WILL GREET THIS DAY WITH A FORGIVING SPIRIT. I WILL FORGIVE MYSELF.

List one person who has wronged you but who, most likely, will never ask forgiveness. What keeps them from asking?

From *The Traveler's Gift* . . .

I cannot recall a single book, including the Holy Bible that says in order for you to forgive someone, he or she has to ask for it. Think about this concept! Where is the rule written that before I forgive people, they have to deserve it? Where is it written that to be forgiven by me, you must have wronged me no more than three times? Or seven? Or seventeen?

_____
_____
_____
_____
_____
_____
_____
_____
_____
_____
_____
_____
_____
_____
_____
_____
_____
_____
_____
_____
_____
_____

I have read the sixth decision for success today.   ☐ A.M.   ☐ P.M.

In applying this decision, today I would give myself a grade of: **A B C D**

I WILL GREET THIS DAY WITH A FORGIVING SPIRIT. I WILL FORGIVE MYSELF.

The person who needs your forgiveness may not even be aware that you've been hurt by them. Or they may have chosen to forget. Either way, it's your choice to give it. Write a short note of your forgiveness to one specific person. It is also your choice whether or not you mail the note.

From *The Traveler's Gift* . . .

T he unmistakable truth about forgiveness is that it is not a reward that must be earned; forgiveness is a gift to be given. When I give forgiveness, I free my own spirit to release the anger and hatred harbored in my heart. By granting forgiveness, I free my spirit to pursue my future happily and unencumbered by the anchors of my past. And forgiveness, when granted to others, becomes a gift to myself.

I have read the sixth decision for success today.   ☐ A.M.   ☐ P.M.

In applying this decision, today I would give myself a grade of: **A B C D**

I WILL GREET THIS DAY WITH A FORGIVING SPIRIT. I WILL FORGIVE MYSELF.

List some areas where you must forgive yourself.

From *The Traveler's Gift* . . .

D avid said. "You're about to go out there, and I'll never see you again. You as much as said my life would be over if I did not forgive this person. So if it's that important, tell me! Who must I forgive?"

The president looked carefully into David's eyes and said simply, "Yourself."

I have read the sixth decision for success today. ☐ A.M. ☐ P.M.

In applying this decision, today I would give myself a grade of: **A B C D**

I WILL GREET THIS DAY WITH A FORGIVING SPIRIT. I WILL FORGIVE MYSELF.

There are many wounded people in the world. And the deepest wound of all is the one we inflict on ourselves. Today is the day to acknowledge that scar, to lay down the guilt, the anger, and the resentment—whatever crime you feel you've committed—and forgive yourself. Will you attempt such a selfless act?

From *The Traveler's Gift . . .*

Tears formed in David's eyes, and he shook his head. Softly, he said, "I didn't think. . ."

"David," Lincoln said as he placed his hands on the younger man's shoulders, "Your wife is not mad at you. Your child is not mad at you. Your friends, of which I am one, are not mad at you, and God is not mad at you. So, David . . . ," Lincoln stopped briefly and said with a smile, "don't you be mad at you. Forgive yourself. Begin anew."

I have read the sixth decision for success today. ☐ A.M. ☐ P.M.

In applying this decision, today I would give myself a grade of: **A B C D**

I WILL GREET THIS DAY WITH A FORGIVING SPIRIT. I WILL FORGIVE MYSELF.

The first great act of creation was separating the light from darkness, day from night. Write out a prayer of dedication to your new beginning.

From *The Traveler's Gift* . . .

B y the simple act of granting forgiveness, I release the demons of the past about which I can do nothing, and I create in myself a new heart, a new beginning.

_____
_____
_____
_____
_____
_____
_____
_____
_____
_____
_____
_____
_____
_____
_____
_____
_____
_____
_____
_____
_____

I have read the sixth decision for success today.   ☐ A.M.   ☐ P.M.

In applying this decision, today I would give myself a grade of: **A B C D**

I WILL GREET THIS DAY WITH A FORGIVING SPIRIT. I WILL FORGIVE MYSELF.

Remember Lot's wife, the one who, when she turned back to look at the city she was fleeing, was turned into a big salt lick? You may be tempted to look back by people who don't care for the 'new, improved you.' What will your response be?

From *The Traveler's Gift* . . .

C riticism is part of the price paid for leaping past mediocrity.

I have read the sixth decision for success today.   ☐ A.M.   ☐ P.M.

In applying this decision, today I would give myself a grade of: **A B C D**

I WILL GREET THIS DAY WITH A FORGIVING SPIRIT. I WILL FORGIVE MYSELF.

Think about the enemy in your head and his strategy for holding you back. Tell him two undeniable truths about the new you.

From *The Traveler's Gift* . . .

I n order to be successful, in all areas of my life, I must control my impulses— my thoughts. It is impossible to fight an enemy living in my head.

I have read the sixth decision for success today. ☐ A.M. ☐ P.M.

In applying this decision, today I would give myself a grade of: **A B C D**

I WILL GREET THIS DAY WITH A FORGIVING SPIRIT. I WILL FORGIVE MYSELF.

You've just aced History by walking out that classroom door.
Where would you like to go on your first day of freedom?

From *The Traveler's Gift* . . .

F rom this day forward,
my history will cease to
control my destiny. I have
forgiven myself. My life has
just begun.

_____

_____

_____

_____

_____

_____

_____

_____

_____

_____

_____

_____

_____

_____

_____

_____

_____

_____

_____

_____

I have read the sixth decision for success today.   ☐ A.M.   ☐ P.M.

In applying this decision, today I would give myself a grade of: **A B C D**

I WILL GREET THIS DAY WITH A FORGIVING SPIRIT. I WILL FORGIVE MYSELF.

The Compassionate Decision
"I Will Greet This Day with a Forgiving Spirit"
Write this decision in your own words.

_____

_____

_____

_____

_____

_____

_____

_____

_____

_____

_____

_____

_____

_____

_____

_____

_____

_____

_____

_____

_____

_____

I have read the sixth decision for success today. ☐ A.M. ☐ P.M.

In applying this decision, today I would give myself a grade of: **A B C D**

I WILL GREET THIS DAY WITH A FORGIVING SPIRIT. I WILL FORGIVE MYSELF.

Now express how this decision will change your life.

_____

_____

_____

_____

_____

_____

_____

_____

_____

_____

_____

_____

_____

_____

_____

_____

_____

_____

_____

_____

_____

I have read the sixth decision for success today. ☐ A.M. ☐ P.M.

In applying this decision, today I would give myself a grade of: **A B C D**

The Persistent Decision for Success

I WILL PERSIST
WITHOUT EXCEPTION.

Knowing that I have already made changes in my life that will last forever, today I insert the final piece of the puzzle. I possess the greatest power ever bestowed upon mankind, the power of choice. Today, I choose to persist without exception. No longer will I live in a dimension of distraction, my focus blown hither and yon like a leaf on a blustery day. I know the outcome I desire. I hold fast to my dreams. I stay the course. I do not quit.

I will persist without exception. I will continue despite exhaustion. I acknowledge that most people quit when exhaustion sets in. I am not "most people." I am stronger than most people. Average people accept exhaustion as a matter of course. I do not. Average people compare themselves with other people. That is why they are average. I compare myself to my potential. I am not average. I see exhaustion as a precursor to victory.

How long must a child try to walk before he actually does so? Do I not have more strength than a child? More understanding? More desire? How long must I work to succeed before I actually do so? A child would never ask the question, for the answer does not matter. By persisting without exception, my outcome—my success—is assured. I will persist without exception. I focus on results.

To achieve the results I desire, it is not even necessary that I enjoy the process. It is only important that I *continue* the process with my eyes on the outcome. An athlete does not enjoy the pain of training; an athlete enjoys the results of having trained. A young falcon is pushed from the nest, afraid and tumbling from the cliff. The pain of learning to fly cannot be an enjoyable experience, but the anguish of learning to fly is quickly forgotten as the falcon soars to the heavens.

A sailor who fearfully watches stormy seas lash his vessel will always steer an unproductive course. But a wise and experienced captain keeps his eye firmly fixed upon the lighthouse. He knows that by guiding his ship directly to a specific point, the time spent in discomfort is lessened. And by keeping his eye on the light, there never exists one second of discouragement. My light, my harbor, my future is within sight!

I will persist without exception. I am a person of great faith. In Jeremiah, my Creator declares, "For I know the plans I have for you, plans to prosper you and not to harm you, plans to give you hope and a future." From this day forward, I will claim a faith in the certainty of my future. Too much of my life has been spent doubting my beliefs and believing my doubts. No more! I have faith in my future. I do not look left or right. I look forward. I can only persist.

For me, faith will always be a sounder guide than reason because reason can only go so far—faith has no limits. I will expect miracles in my life because faith produces them every day. I will believe in the future that I do not see. That is faith. And the reward of this faith is to see the future that I believed.

I will continue despite exhaustion.

I focus on results.

I am a person of great faith.

I will persist without exception.

I WILL PERSIST WITHOUT EXCEPTION. I AM A PERSON OF GREAT FAITH.

So, which is it? 20% faith with 80% fear?
Or the other way around?

From *The Traveler's Gift* . . .

G abriel's eyebrows rose. "A simple question actually. Do you consider yourself a man of faith? Does faith guide your everyday actions and emotions? All men are driven by faith or fear—one or the other—for both are the same. Faith or fear is the expectation of an event that hasn't come to pass or the belief in something that cannot be seen or touched. A man of fear lives always on the edge of insanity. A man of faith lives in perpetual reward."

I have read the seventh decision for success today.   ☐ A.M.   ☐ P.M.

In applying this decision, today I would give myself a grade of: **A B C D**

I WILL PERSIST WITHOUT EXCEPTION. I AM A PERSON OF GREAT FAITH.

Which areas of your life are the most fearful?
In which areas do you rest in faith?

_____

_____

_____

_____

_____

_____

_____

_____

_____

_____

_____

_____

_____

_____

_____

_____

_____

_____

_____

_____

I have read the seventh decision for success today.   ☐ A.M.   ☐ P.M.

In applying this decision, today I would give myself a grade of: **A B C D**

I WILL PERSIST WITHOUT EXCEPTION. I AM A PERSON OF GREAT FAITH.

There is a point in the universe that reason cannot touch. Beyond that, is hope. What doubts cloud your view of where hope lives?

From *The Traveler's Gift . . .*

Walking again, Gabriel replied, "Faith is to believe what one has not seen. The reward of faith is to see what one has believed. Do you consider yourself a man of faith, David Ponder?"

"To be honest," David replied, "I have always thought of myself as a man of reason."

Gabriel turned right, leading his guest down a wide aisle. "Reason never makes room for miracles; faith releases miracles. And in final comparison, faith is a sounder guide than reason. Reason can only be stretched so far, but faith has no limits. The only limit to your realization of tomorrow is the doubt to which you hold fast today."

I have read the seventh decision for success today. ☐ A.M. ☐ P.M.

In applying this decision, today I would give myself a grade of: **A B C D**

I WILL PERSIST WITHOUT EXCEPTION. I AM A PERSON OF GREAT FAITH.

Think about this for 30 seconds and then answer:
How do you define 'circumstances'?

From *The Traveler's Gift* . . .

W hat is the difference
in people, David
Ponder," the angel began,
"when they hit despair?
Why does one person take
his own life while another
moves to greatness?"

"That didn't answer my
question," David replied,
"but I'm not sure. I've never
really thought about it."

Gabriel turned, still
walking, with a mildly
amused look on his face.
"Think about it now," he
said simply.

David shrugged. "I don't
know. Maybe it's a
difference in
circumstances."

I have read the seventh decision for success today.   ☐ A.M.   ☐ P.M.

In applying this decision, today I would give myself a grade of: **A B C D**

I WILL PERSIST WITHOUT EXCEPTION. I AM A PERSON OF GREAT FAITH.

How much do 'circumstances' weigh in your life right now?

_____

_____

_____

_____

_____

_____

_____

_____

_____

_____

_____

_____

_____

_____

_____

_____

_____

_____

_____

_____

I have read the seventh decision for success today.   ☐ A.M.   ☐ P.M.

In applying this decision, today I would give myself a grade of: **A B C D**

I WILL PERSIST WITHOUT EXCEPTION. I AM A PERSON OF GREAT FAITH.

Take the stuff of your life and rearrange the room.
What needs to be packed away? What needs to go to the trash?
What could be refurbished?

From *The Traveler's Gift* . . .

C ircumstances do not push or pull. They are daily lessons to be studied and gleaned for new knowledge and wisdom. Knowledge and wisdom that is applied will bring about a brighter tomorrow. A person who is depressed is spending too much time thinking about the way things are now and not enough time thinking about how he wants things to be.

I have read the seventh decision for success today.   ☐ A.M.   ☐ P.M.

In applying this decision, today I would give myself a grade of: **A B C D**

I WILL PERSIST WITHOUT EXCEPTION. I AM A PERSON OF GREAT FAITH.

What daily lessons do you need to remind yourself of often?
Which circumstances have brought about a great deal
of wisdom and knowledge?

_____

_____

_____

_____

_____

_____

_____

_____

_____

_____

_____

_____

_____

_____

_____

_____

_____

_____

I have read the seventh decision for success today.   ☐ A.M.   ☐ P.M.

In applying this decision, today I would give myself a grade of: **A B C D**

Winners never quit. Quitters never win. When was the last time you should've won but you didn't? Why didn't you?

From *The Traveler's Gift* . . .

G abriel smiled and sat down beside David on the floor. "You must know," he began, "that in the game of life, nothing is less important than the score at halftime. The tragedy of life is not that man loses, but that he almost wins."

David shook his head slowly. "Why do we quit? Why do I quit? Why do I ease off? Why do I detour everything in my life?"

Gabriel responded instantly, "As a human, you detour and ease off because you lack understanding. You quit because you lack faith."

I have read the seventh decision for success today.   ☐ A.M.   ☐ P.M.

In applying this decision, today I would give myself a grade of: **A B C D**

I WILL PERSIST WITHOUT EXCEPTION. I AM A PERSON OF GREAT FAITH.

Why is it impossible for quitters to win?

_____

_____

_____

_____

_____

_____

_____

_____

_____

_____

_____

_____

_____

_____

_____

_____

_____

_____

_____

_____

I have read the seventh decision for success today.   ☐ A.M.   ☐ P.M.

In applying this decision, today I would give myself a grade of: **A B C D**

I WILL PERSIST WITHOUT EXCEPTION. I AM A PERSON OF GREAT FAITH.

Name your giants, the obstacles in between you and success?

From *The Traveler's Gift* . . .

Y ou do not understand
that constant detours
do not bring a man into the
presence of greatness.
Detours do not build
muscle. Detours do not
provide life's lessons.
Between you and anything
significant will be giants in
your path.

I have read the seventh decision for success today.   ☐ A.M.   ☐ P.M.

In applying this decision, today I would give myself a grade of: **A B C D**

I WILL PERSIST WITHOUT EXCEPTION. I AM A PERSON OF GREAT FAITH.

Now think about the story of David and Goliath.
What kind of 'stones' might fell those giants?

_____

_____

_____

_____

_____

_____

_____

_____

_____

_____

_____

_____

_____

_____

_____

_____

_____

_____

_____

_____

_____

I have read the seventh decision for success today. ☐ A.M. ☐ P.M.

In applying this decision, today I would give myself a grade of: **A B C D**

I WILL PERSIST WITHOUT EXCEPTION. I AM A PERSON OF GREAT FAITH.

What doesn't kill us makes us stronger. Makes us greater. How much longer can you take the heat?

From *The Traveler's Gift* . . .

Times of calamity and distress have always been producers of the greatest men. The hardest steel is produced from the hottest fire; the brightest star shreds the darkest night.

I have read the seventh decision for success today.   ☐ A.M.   ☐ P.M.

In applying this decision, today I would give myself a grade of: **A B C D**

I WILL PERSIST WITHOUT EXCEPTION. I AM A PERSON OF GREAT FAITH.

What bright star has come into your life
to shred the darkest night?

_____

_____

_____

_____

_____

_____

_____

_____

_____

_____

_____

_____

_____

_____

_____

_____

_____

_____

_____

_____

_____

_____

_____

I have read the seventh decision for success today.   ☐ A.M.   ☐ P.M.

In applying this decision, today I would give myself a grade of: **A B C D**

I WILL PERSIST WITHOUT EXCEPTION. I AM A PERSON OF GREAT FAITH.

Imagine for a second that, in a jungle full of amazing creatures, you are the rarest and most extraordinary bird of all. You will only grow more valuable with each passing year. Describe how that might feel.

From *The Traveler's Gift* . . .

A verage people compare themselves to other people. That is why they are average. I compare myself to my potential. I am not average. I see exhaustion as a precursor to victory.

I have read the seventh decision for success today.   ☐ A.M.   ☐ P.M.

In applying this decision, today I would give myself a grade of: **A B C D**

I WILL PERSIST WITHOUT EXCEPTION. I AM A PERSON OF GREAT FAITH.

Who do you compare yourself to on a regular basis?
Why that person?

_____

_____

_____

_____

_____

_____

_____

_____

_____

_____

_____

_____

_____

_____

_____

_____

_____

_____

_____

_____

_____

I have read the seventh decision for success today.   ☐ A.M.   ☐ P.M.

In applying this decision, today I would give myself a grade of: **A B C D**

I WILL PERSIST WITHOUT EXCEPTION. I AM A PERSON OF GREAT FAITH.

Every journey begins with one step. Sometimes each step that follows get easier; sometimes the terrain makes each step nearly impossible. What matters is that you keep stepping. How difficult is the next step on your journey?

From *The Traveler's Gift*...

How long must a child try to walk before he actually does so? Do I have more strength than a child? More understanding? More desire? How long must I work to succeed before I actually do so? A child would never ask the question, for the answer does not matter. By persisting without exception, my outcome— my success—is assured.

I have read the seventh decision for success today.   ☐ A.M.   ☐ P.M.

In applying this decision, today I would give myself a grade of: **A B C D**

I WILL PERSIST WITHOUT EXCEPTION. I AM A PERSON OF GREAT FAITH.

Identify for yourself those next steps that need to be taken in your journey.

_____

_____

_____

_____

_____

_____

_____

_____

_____

_____

_____

_____

_____

_____

_____

_____

_____

_____

_____

_____

_____

I have read the seventh decision for success today. ☐ A.M. ☐ P.M.

In applying this decision, today I would give myself a grade of: **A B C D**

I WILL PERSIST WITHOUT EXCEPTION. I AM A PERSON OF GREAT FAITH.

Do you buy into the theory of 'no pain, no gain'? Why or why not?

From *The Traveler's Gift* . . .

An athlete does not enjoy the pain of training; an athlete enjoys the results of having trained.

I have read the seventh decision for success today.   ☐ A.M.   ☐ P.M.

In applying this decision, today I would give myself a grade of: **A B C D**

I WILL PERSIST WITHOUT EXCEPTION. I AM A PERSON OF GREAT FAITH.

Remind yourself of a time when great pain brought great gain in your life.

_____

_____

_____

_____

_____

_____

_____

_____

_____

_____

_____

_____

_____

_____

_____

_____

_____

_____

_____

_____

_____

_____

I have read the seventh decision for success today. ☐ A.M. ☐ P.M.

In applying this decision, today I would give myself a grade of: **A B C D**

I WILL PERSIST WITHOUT EXCEPTION. I AM A PERSON OF GREAT FAITH.

Describe a time in your life when you felt free as the flying falcon that roams the heavens.

From *The Traveler's Gift* . . .

A young falcon is pushed from the nest, afraid and tumbling from the cliff. The pain of learning to fly cannot be an enjoyable experience, but the anguish of learning to fly is quickly forgotten as the falcon soars to the heavens.

I have read the seventh decision for success today.   ☐ A.M.   ☐ P.M.

In applying this decision, today I would give myself a grade of: **A B C D**

I WILL PERSIST WITHOUT EXCEPTION. I AM A PERSON OF GREAT FAITH.

What made you feel free to fly?

_____

_____

_____

_____

_____

_____

_____

_____

_____

_____

_____

_____

_____

_____

_____

_____

_____

_____

_____

_____

_____

I have read the seventh decision for success today. ☐ A.M. ☐ P.M.

In applying this decision, today I would give myself a grade of: **A B C D**

I WILL PERSIST WITHOUT EXCEPTION. I AM A PERSON OF GREAT FAITH.

The Persistent Decision
"I Will Persist Without Exception"
Write this decision in your own words.

_____

_____

_____

_____

_____

_____

_____

_____

_____

_____

_____

_____

_____

_____

_____

_____

_____

_____

_____

_____

_____

I have read the seventh decision for success today.   ☐ A.M.   ☐ P.M.

In applying this decision, today I would give myself a grade of: **A B C D**

I WILL PERSIST WITHOUT EXCEPTION. I AM A PERSON OF GREAT FAITH.

Now express how this decision will change your life.

_____

_____

_____

_____

_____

_____

_____

_____

_____

_____

_____

_____

_____

_____

_____

_____

_____

_____

_____

_____

_____

_____

I have read the seventh decision for success today.   ☐ A.M.   ☐ P.M.

In applying this decision, today I would give myself a grade of: **A B C D**

The Traveler's Gift

TODAY I START
MY NEW LIFE.

My family will be fine. Our future is assured. I will make it so.

Do you feel you understand the meaning of the Seven Decisions for Success? What decision stands out the most for you?

From *The Traveler's Gift* . . .

I t was a simple choice really. A choice made under duress. But now, of course, our lives have been transformed—financially, emotionally, spiritually— literally transformed in every way. My family has been set free. You see, it wasn't enough that I possessed the Seven Decisions for Success or even that I understood their meaning. The moment I decided to make them a part of my life was the moment that the future of my family was secured for generations.

I have read the decisions for success today. ☐ A.M. ☐ P.M.

In applying this decision, today I would give myself a grade of: **A B C D**

My family will be fine. Our future is assured. I will make it so.

What would it take for you to make the Seven Decisions for Success a real, lasting part of your life?

_____

_____

_____

_____

_____

_____

_____

_____

_____

_____

_____

_____

_____

_____

_____

_____

_____

I have read the decisions for success today.   ☐ A.M.   ☐ P.M.

In applying this decision, today I would give myself a grade of: **A B C D**

MY FAMILY WILL BE FINE. OUR FUTURE IS ASSURED. I WILL MAKE IT SO.

*Beyond your present thoughts and actions . . . a future beyond
today. When you think about those words, what do you envision?*

From *The Traveler's Gift* . . .

We know now the gift
of the possibility of
success for anyone. . . . I am
here to challenge you to
grasp a future that is far
beyond your present
thoughts and actions.

I have read the decisions for success today.   ☐ A.M.   ☐ P.M.

In applying this decision, today I would give myself a grade of: **A B C D**

My family will be fine. Our future is assured. I will make it so.

Are you going to grasp that future?
What level of commitment is behind that decision?

_____

_____

_____

_____

_____

_____

_____

_____

_____

_____

_____

_____

_____

_____

_____

_____

_____

_____

_____

I have read the decisions for success today.   ☐ A.M.   ☐ P.M.

In applying this decision, today I would give myself a grade of: **A B C D**

MY FAMILY WILL BE FINE. OUR FUTURE IS ASSURED. I WILL MAKE IT SO.

Everyone leaves a legacy, a life that impacts generations of people for better or worse. What kind of legacy will you leave?

From *The Traveler's Gift* . . .

There comes a time in every person's life when a decision is required. And that decision, should you make it, will have a far-reaching effect on generations yet unborn.

_____

I have read the decisions for success today. ☐ A.M. ☐ P.M.

In applying this decision, today I would give myself a grade of: **A B C D**

My family will be fine. Our future is assured. I will make it so.

*What decisions are required of you today in order
to leave the legacy you desire?*

I have read the decisions for success today.   ☐ A.M.   ☐ P.M.

In applying this decision, today I would give myself a grade of: **A B C D**

My family will be fine. Our future is assured. I will make it so.

Think back over the course of your life. Trace your steps and write about one choice that changed the trajectory of your life. One powerful, life-changing choice.

From *The Traveler's Gift* . . .

There is a thin thread that weaves only from you to hundreds of thousands of lives. Your example, your actions, and yes, even one decision can literally change the world. Let me say that one more time. One decision, that you make, can literally change the world.

_____

I have read the decisions for success today. ☐ A.M. ☐ P.M.

In applying this decision, today I would give myself a grade of: **A B C D**

My family will be fine. Our future is assured. I will make it so.

Do you see a need to make another life-changing choice in the near future? What advice would you share with others facing a life-changing choice?

_____

_____

_____

_____

_____

_____

_____

_____

_____

_____

_____

_____

_____

_____

_____

_____

_____

_____

_____

I have read the decisions for success today.   ☐ A.M.   ☐ P.M.

In applying this decision, today I would give myself a grade of: **A B C D**

My family will be fine. Our future is assured. I will make it so.

One man's actions resulted in a victory that changed the course of history. Something you do this very day could do the same for a complete stranger. Think about the possibilities and write your thoughts.

From *The Traveler's Gift* . . .

H ad the South been victorious at Gettysburg, historians agree that the entire conflict would have been over by the end of the summer. The Confederate States of America were one victory away from winning the war. But they didn't win.

I have read the decisions for success today. ☐ A.M. ☐ P.M.

In applying this decision, today I would give myself a grade of: **A B C D**

MY FAMILY WILL BE FINE. OUR FUTURE IS ASSURED. I WILL MAKE IT SO.

Are you a 'Plain Jane'? Weak? Ordinary? Great!
Because God always uses the "least likely to . . ."
to accomplish great things. Are you willing?

From *The Traveler's Gift* . . .

The schoolteacher from Maine was awarded the Congressional Medal of Honor for his decision at Little Round Top. His commanding officers determined that the actions of this one man saved the Union army from being destroyed—this one man turned the tide of the battle. Joshua Lawrence Chamberlain turned the tide of the war. . . . Because one ordinary man made a decision to move forward, this is a very different world we live in today. . . .

I have read the decisions for success today.   ☐ A.M.   ☐ P.M.

In applying this decision, today I would give myself a grade of: **A B C D**

MY FAMILY WILL BE FINE. OUR FUTURE IS ASSURED. I WILL MAKE IT SO.

One decision. One simple decision. Start with the decision to love.
What might that mean in your life?

From *The Traveler's Gift* . . .

D on't you ever think
that you can't change
things! You can! You can!
One decision, that you
make, can change the
world!

I have read the decisions for success today.   ☐ A.M.   ☐ P.M.

In applying this decision, today I would give myself a grade of: **A B C D**

My family will be fine. Our future is assured. I will make it so.

Who else would be affected by your decision to love?
How could that change a piece of your world?

I have read the decisions for success today.   ☐ A.M.   ☐ P.M.

In applying this decision, today I would give myself a grade of: **A B C D**

MY FAMILY WILL BE FINE. OUR FUTURE IS ASSURED. I WILL MAKE IT SO.

A true leader serves those she leads by seeking their success as much as her own. Think of one thing you can do today to help someone succeed. Write it down.

From *The Traveler's Gift* . . .

It is a fact that people follow a man who simply says, 'Follow me.' By taking leadership, ironically, a person deserves leadership. As you lead others to success and a life of their dreams, the life you seek and deserve will be revealed unto you.

I have read the decisions for success today. ☐ A.M. ☐ P.M.

In applying this decision, today I would give myself a grade of: **A B C D**

MY FAMILY WILL BE FINE. OUR FUTURE IS ASSURED. I WILL MAKE IT SO.

Who helped you to succeed through their leadership?
Did you ever thank them for that leadership?
What should you say to them?

_____

_____

_____

_____

_____

_____

_____

_____

_____

_____

_____

_____

_____

_____

_____

_____

_____

_____

_____

_____

I have read the decisions for success today.   ☐ A.M.   ☐ P.M.

In applying this decision, today I would give myself a grade of: **A B C D**

MY FAMILY WILL BE FINE. OUR FUTURE IS ASSURED. I WILL MAKE IT SO.

*Have you sensed a hedge of thorns in your life? Describe a
specific time when you experienced divine protection.*

From *The Traveler's Gift* . . .

I ncidentally, an
interesting benefit of a
person's decision to charge,
one that has been
somewhat overlooked by
scholars and historians, is
the presence of a hedge of
thorns. Mentioned first in
the Bible, a hedge of thorns
is the divine protection
placed upon a person who is
destined to make a
difference. Until you have
accomplished what you
were put here to do, you
will not—you cannot—be
harmed.

I have read the decisions for success today.   ☐ A.M.   ☐ P.M.

In applying this decision, today I would give myself a grade of: **A B C D**

MY FAMILY WILL BE FINE. OUR FUTURE IS ASSURED. I WILL MAKE IT SO.

"Get busy living, or get busy dying," Andy Dufresne tells his fellow convict and friend, Red, in the movie The Shawshank Redemption. Put that admonition in your own words and personalize it as a reminder to yourself to keep moving forward.

From *The Traveler's Gift . . .*

Failure is the only possible result of a life that accepts the status quo. We move forward or we die!

I have read the decisions for success today.   ☐ A.M.   ☐ P.M.

In applying this decision, today I would give myself a grade of: **A B C D**

My family will be fine. Our future is assured. I will make it so.

Remind yourself of failures that are now in the past. Now remind yourself of ways you are moving forward away from those failures.

From *The Traveler's Gift* . . .

Your story, your circumstances, your timing may not be as dramatic as those of Joshua Chamberlain, but the stakes are exactly the same. There comes a time in every person's life when a decision is required. And that decision, should you make it, will have a far-reaching effect on generations yet unborn. There is a thin thread that weaves from only you to hundreds of thousands of lives. Your example, your actions, and yes, even one decision that you make will literally change the world.

I have read the decisions for success today. ☐ A.M. ☐ P.M.

In applying this decision, today I would give myself a grade of: **A B C D**

My family will be fine. Our future is assured. I will make it so.

So what decisions are required in your life?
What is the far-reaching effect?

_____

_____

_____

_____

_____

_____

_____

_____

_____

_____

_____

_____

_____

_____

_____

_____

_____

_____

_____

I have read the decisions for success today.   ☐ A.M.   ☐ P.M.

In applying this decision, today I would give myself a grade of: **A B C D**

My family will be fine. Our future is assured. I will make it so.

What motivation are you going to use each day to "charge" ahead in life?

From *The Traveler's Gift . . .*

So do it. Change your life. Change your family's future. Change the world. Charge. Charge. Charge.

_____

_____

_____

_____

_____

_____

_____

_____

_____

_____

_____

_____

_____

_____

_____

_____

_____

_____

_____

I have read the decisions for success today.   ☐ A.M.   ☐ P.M.

In applying this decision, today I would give myself a grade of: **A B C D**

MY FAMILY WILL BE FINE. OUR FUTURE IS ASSURED. I WILL MAKE IT SO.

In what ways are you going to change
your family's future for the better?

_____

_____

_____

_____

_____

_____

_____

_____

_____

_____

_____

_____

_____

_____

_____

_____

_____

_____

_____

I have read the decisions for success today.   ☐ A.M.   ☐ P.M.

In applying this decision, today I would give myself a grade of: **A B C D**

MY FAMILY WILL BE FINE. OUR FUTURE IS ASSURED. I WILL MAKE IT SO.

What example do you wish to leave for future generations?
In what ways do you wish to change the world?

_____

_____

_____

_____

_____

_____

_____

_____

_____

_____

_____

_____

_____

_____

_____

_____

_____

_____

I have read the decisions for success today.   ☐ A.M.   ☐ P.M.

In applying this decision, today I would give myself a grade of: **A B C D**

Seven Decisions
That Determine Personal Success

1. The buck stops here. I am responsible for my past and my future.

2. I will seek wisdom. I will be a servant to others.

3. I am a person of action. I seize this moment. I choose now.

4. I have a decided heart. My destiny is assured.

5. Today I will choose to be happy. I am the possessor of a grateful spirit.

6. I will greet this day with a forgiving spirit. I will forgive myself.

7. I will persist without exception. I am a person of great faith.

I will be fine.

My family will be fine.

Our future is assured.

I will make it so.

When you speak or write these words, you breathe them into existence as a truth on which this day—this week, this month, this year . . . YOUR life—will turn. Speak and write them often. Now Charge!—full speed ahead—into the future of your dreams!